ON AUTHORITY

ON AUTHORITY

A PHILOSOPHICAL DIALOGUE

Nicholas J. Pappas

Algora Publishing
New York

Library of Congress Cataloging-in-Publication Data —

Names: Pappas, Nicholas J., author.
Title: On authority : a philosophical dialogue / Nicholas J. Pappas.
Description: New York : Algora Publishing, [2021] | Summary: "A
    philosophical treatment of the idea of authority, this book is a
    dialogue between three characters. "Director," a philosopher, challenges
    the others to think through their ideas of authority, how it is
    established, how it works, and how it can be either subtle or bold"--
    Provided by publisher.
Identifiers: LCCN 2021042495 (print) | LCCN 2021042496 (ebook) | ISBN
    9781628944730 (trade paperback) | ISBN 9781628944747 (hardcover) | ISBN
    9781628944754 (pdf)
Subjects: LCSH: Authority.
Classification: LCC BD209 .P37 2021 (print) | LCC BD209 (ebook) | DDC
    121/.6--dc23
LC record available at https://lccn.loc.gov/2021042495
LC ebook record available at https://lccn.loc.gov/2021042496

Printed in the United States

More Books by Nick Pappas
from Algora Publishing

Controvert, or On the Lie and Other Philosophical Dialogues, 2008

Aristocrat, and The Community: Two Philosophical Dialogues, 2010

On Awareness: A Collection of Philosophical Dialogues, 2011

Belief and Integrity: Philosophical Dialogues, 2011

On Strength, 2012

On Freedom: A Philosophical Dialogue, 2014

On Life: Philosophical Dialogues, 2015

On Love: A Philosophical Dialogue, 2016

On Destiny: A Philosophical Dialogue, 2016

On Wisdom: A Philosophical Dialogue, 2017

All of Health: A Philosophical Dialogue, 2018

On Education: A Philosophical Dialogue, 2018

On Power: A Philosophical Dialogue, 2019

On Ideas: A Philosophical Dialogue, 2020

On Passivity: A Philosophical Dialogue, 2021

Introduction

In this book I present a politician, a general, and a philosopher in conversation. This chance meeting finds them with unexpected time on their hands, a hiatus from the everyday pressures, a rare chance for a spontaneous conversation with interesting partners. The meeting had to happen by chance. The blizzard was the opportunity. Much of philosophy depends on chance, on making the most of it.

By chance, or the philosopher's steering, the three hit on authority as their theme for the three hours or so they talk. Both the politician and the general are authority figures. The philosopher, Director, is not. And yet the two authorities come to treat him as one, on an equal footing with them. How does this happen?

As the book ends, the three discuss the extent to which a mob has authority when it rules. It seems not all 'authorities' are authorities. The difference is both moral and practical. Articulating this difference is the major work of this book.

I'll close with a quote from the middle of the conversation:

Director: [...] Do you know of any authorities who can't stand on their own two feet?

Politician: No, authorities always stand on their own two feet.

General: Except when they're using others as crutches.

Politician: Yes, but then they're 'authorities,' not authorities.

Director: You're suggesting something radical.

Politician: Oh?

Director: We obey authorities, but we don't obey 'authorities.'

[...]

General: In the military you sometimes find 'authorities.' But you have to obey them nonetheless. So I'd say that you civilians, given the freedom you have, should disobey as often as you can. That way, eventually, we'll have good leadership at our head.

Enjoy,
Nick Pappas

On Authority

CHARACTERS: *Politician, Director, General*

SCENE: *Hotel Lounge*

1

Politician: What a blizzard! All flights canceled.

General: We were lucky to make it here before the roads got really bad.

Politician: I suppose there are worse places to be stuck. I love the dark wood in here. And that fire!

General: I have to admit, this leather chair feels good. It's been a long day.

Politician: I thought you did a great job testifying before the committee.

General: Thank you. Goodness knows I prepared. But let's not talk shop.

Director: Sorry. I'll move so you two can have some privacy.

Politician: No! We wouldn't think of it. Stay where you are. We have the three best seats in the house. So what brought you to the capital?

Director: I was a last minute substitute for my boss. I gave a pitch.

Politician: Ah, a salesman.

Director: No, I'm in operations.

Politician: Then why did your boss have you give a pitch?

Director: Our company consults on operations.

Politician: Well, we're all in sales these days.

Director: What do you sell?

Politician: Ideas. So does General. He sells the idea of his troops. But he could use some help with his marketing.

General: I've never really understood the difference between marketing and sales.

Director: Marketing spreads the net...

Politician: ...and sales pulls it tight to catch the prey!

Director: General, what's your prey?

Politician: I'll answer that since he seems unsure. Dollars, my friend. Dollars.

Director: Dollars controlled by politicians?

Politician: Yes. Certain politicians hold the cash, while others make a pitch to have it.

Director: What sort of politician are you? A holder or a pitcher?

Politician: I'm something of an authority as both a holder and a pitcher.

Director: You're an authority on either side of the game? Is that rare?

Politician: Not so rare to play both roles. What's rare is to play those roles well.

Director: And when you do, you're an authority on the game as a whole?

Politician: Yes. And if I say so myself, no one in the House is more of an authority than I. But here, let's have another drink.

2

Politician: You're right to call it a game. The game of authority. Here's one of its twists. I can be a tremendous authority in Congress, but when I go back home I have to be on an equal footing with my constituents.

General: I don't have that twist. I stay an authority through and through. My job demands it.

Director: My job's the same.

Politician: How so?

Director: My expertise makes me an authority with both those inside and, sometimes, outside the company.

General: Then you have more authority than I do. I once went outside the company, so to speak, to a college to give a speech. I'll tell you, not all those students saw me as an authority to respect!

Director: But they saw you as an authority, nonetheless.

General: True. But what about you, Politician? Is your 'company' Congress?

Politician: And my home state is my 'campus'? You must be kidding, General. My home state is my home!

General: But you can't be too much of an authority at home, or the voters will turn on you. When— Sorry, what's your name?

Director: Director.

General: When Director and I are at home, we exercise our full authority. Very different things.

Politician: Tell us something, Director. What is authority?

Director: I like to think of it as involving a looking up to someone or something. There are two types of authority, in my view. Voluntary and involuntary.

General: You mean some people are involuntarily authorities?

Director: Yes, I think that's true. But I was thinking of something else. There are those we look up to because we want to, and there are those we look up to because we're forced.

Politician: General knows all about the latter.

General: Bad generals know all about the latter. Good generals generate good will.

Politician: But still, they need force from time to time.

General: Oh, of course. Force is the background in what I do—and often enough in the foreground, too. What about you, Director? Do you need force?

Director: I make use of the force of reason. I articulate what I know in a way that people can appreciate and understand. Does this make me an authority?

Politician: Sure, but there's all the difference in the world between the force of reason and the force of law, or the force of... force.

Director: But Politician, surely you make use of the force of reason every day.

Politician: I do! What do you think debate is? It's nothing but reason.

General: Not if you make sneaky arguments.

Politician: Director, tell the general the truth about sneaky arguments.

Director: The truth is that there can be as much reason in sneaking around as in making a frontal attack.

Politician: Yes! And oftentimes more.

General: Says the crafty politician.

Politician: Would you rather be represented by the dim of wit? Director?

Director: No, you have a point. But where do you direct your craft?

Politician: Toward other politicians.

Director: Is that the source of your authority?

Politician: My source is when I get things done.

Director: And that's how you get your authority, however limited, at home?

Politician: Of course. My constituents respect a job well done.

Director: Hmm.

General: What is it?

Director: Does authority always demand respect?

General: I know I do. And you?

Director: I don't.

Politician: You need to up your game.

Director: Can't I be an authority with whatever respect I happen to earn, not demand?

Politician: I suppose—something of an authority, at least. But authority isn't all that's at stake.

Director: Oh? What's at stake?

Politician: Power.

Director: Power?

Politician: Oh, don't play dumb. Authority and power are closely linked. If you want power, you'd do well to have as much respect as you can command.

General: He has a point.

Director: But can't you have power without respect?

Politician: Sure, in a tyranny.

General: But even there people are forced to pretend they have respect.

Director: Because the tyrant demands it?

General: Yes.

Politician: And that's the problem. It's better to command than demand. Demanding makes you seem... petulant.

3

Director: Do tyrants demand respect everywhere they turn?

Politician: That's what makes them tyrannical.

Director: And if they commanded respect everywhere they turned?

Politician: That might make them kings.

General: Oh, but be serious. No one can force respect. Some will respect us; some won't. That's all we can say.

Director: Tell us, Politician. Will those who don't respect you vote for you?

Politician: Probably not.

Director: And those who respect you will?

Politician: For the most part, yes.

Director: So your game is all about respect.

Politician: But so is everyone's.

Director: Really? General, will those who don't respect you obey your commands?

General: They absolutely will.

Director: Seems like a different game to me.

Politician: Then tell us, Director. Do you ever issue commands?

Director: I ask people to do things.

Politician: Do you give them reasons why?

Director: I do.

Politician: But it's still a command.

Director: Not really. They might tell me why my reasons aren't good. If they can explain a better course, that's the course we'll take.

General: Well, yes. That's what I do with my staff. I'm no tyrant, Politician.

Politician: I never thought you were. But even so, it's good to have Congressional oversight. You're not the only general in the land.

Director: Because Congress is always so reasonable?

Politician: Congress is almost never reasonable. But individual congresspeople are, or can be. And that has to be enough.

Director: So if you want to sell, sell to those of reason?

Politician: If you're a good salesman, that's what you try to do.

General: Director, you were selling today. How did it go?

Director: I think it went okay.

General: Do you think you made the sale?

Director: I can't tell. My boss would be better at answering that.

General: Why didn't he come?

Director: He's afraid to travel in bad weather.

General: He told you this?

Director: No, but I've seen a pattern over the years.

General: What was his excuse?

Director: He said his cat was sick.

General: Was his cat sick?

Director: Yes, I think so.

General: But you said he was afraid of bad weather.

Director: Yes, but if he dies in a plane crash, who will take care of his cat?

Politician: Ha! You really believe that's a good reason not to come?

Director: It's a reason. How good a reason is up to my boss.

General: You respect your boss's love for his cat.

Director: Of course. I love my cats, too.

4

Politician: Tell us, General. Is your army made up of dogs or cats?

General: The bulk are dogs, with special units of cats.

Politician: Is that how armies have always been?

General: I think so, yes.

Politician: Why?

General: Because dogs obey, or can be taught to obey.

Politician: And cats?

General: They need special handling.

Politician: And when they're handled well?

General: They round out the force.

Director: Do dogs respect you more than cats?

General: In general? They probably do. But once you win the respect of a cat, very good things can happen.

Politician: How do you win the respect of a cat?

General: Oh, you know how. Congress has cats. But I'll tell you. You have to show them respect. And be firm when they cross the line.

Politician: How does that differ from dogs? You don't have to show them respect? Or are they easier to deal with when they cross the line?

General: Let me put it this way. Most cats need their space; most dogs love to be close at hand. This difference calls for different kinds of discipline and respect.

Politician: Discipline is discipline, and respect is respect. Director?

Director: What I want to know, General, is whether you visit your dogs regularly.

General: Often, and gladly.

Director: Do you wait for your cats to come and visit you?

General: You know, in a sense, I do. I wait for a sign that I'm needed. We have an understanding that way.

Director: With whom is your authority greater?

General: If I do it right? It's equal.

Politician: Oh, come on! You know it's with the dogs.

General: Maybe. But with whom is your authority greater? With Congress or those back home? What, no answer?

Director: But, General, he's told us his problem, his paradox. He gains authority by treating his voters as equals.

Politician: But they are my equals.

General: Nonsense. Some of them are, I'm sure. But really? Equals? You have great cleverness and skill. Not all do. So not all are equal. Do you deny it?

Politician: We're all equal before the law.

General: That we are, mostly. And to you each of them is one vote. Equal, because you're a vote, too.

Director: Each vote has authority in this our land.

General: You're the first person I've heard say that. And it's profoundly true. Each is an authority on how they'll cast their vote. Each must be respected for that vote. This is by law; by force, if you will.

Politician: No one forces me to respect my constituents. I respect them by choice.

General: You respect them by ambition.

Politician: True. But my ambition is to serve.

5

Politician: Do you serve?

General: Do I serve? Are you serious? I serve my country and my troops.

Politician: So we're essentially the same.

General: What do you serve, Director?

Director: I serve philosophy.

Politician: What? Ha, ha. What are you talking about?

General: He said he serves philosophy. How, Director?

Director: By having conversations like this.

Politician: What good comes of this other than killing time?

Director: The time you want to kill I see as opportunity.

Politician: Opportunity for what?

Director: To learn.

Politician: And what are you learning about? Authority?

Director: Yes.

Politician: What have you learned so far?

Director: That your authority is more difficult to master than General's and mine.

General: I'd like to see him try to lead an army in battle.

Politician: I'd like to see you mount an electoral campaign.

Director: My job seems easy compared to both of yours.

General: But why do you think his is harder?

Director: You can always be one and the same, even with your cats. Politician has to be many to many.

Politician: It's true. I'm a sort of chameleon.

General: What's hard about that?

Politician: Remembering who you are.

General: Ha! If you have trouble with that, how can you lead?

Politician: The people tell me where to go. And then they follow me there.

Director: Is that how generals lead?

General: What, my soldiers tell me where to go? No, of course not. Mine is a lonely command. I set the course then lead the way.

Politician: Hoping everyone follows.

General: That's your hope. My hope is that I know where I'm going—and that I'll know what to do when I'm there. What's your hope, Director?

Director: I hope I'm the best philosopher I can be.

Politician: Oh, what's with this philosophy stuff? What does it take to be a good philosopher?

General: I know what it takes. Love.

Politician: Ha! And why do you think that?

General: Because I studied the art and philosophy of war in command college. And my teacher always liked to quip, 'All's fair in war... and love!'

Politician: Ha, ha. Okay, true. So, philosopher, is that what you know? That all is fair?

Director: In anything? Or just in love and war?

Politician: Between the two we have most everything covered, I think.

Director: So the question is whether we can accomplish our ends, whatever end, by any means. Well, my answer is yes.

General: You don't mean that.

Director: But I do.

Politician: You'd be willing to lie and cheat and steal?

Director: No, because those things generally won't help me achieve my ends.

General: What are your ends?

Director: I'll tell you one. I want to make friends.

General: Well, you're making some here tonight.

Director: Then I'm grateful for the storm.

General: I am, too. It's good to have a break now and then. Goodness knows we keep up a killer pace. Does your boss drive you hard?

Director: He lets me set my own pace. He's concerned with results.

Politician: And you deliver.

Director: I do.

General: What's the secret to your success?

Director: I make it a point to know my business and listen to my team.

General: That's the secret to my success. And you, Politician?

Politician: The same—with the added variable of the People.

Director: What do you do if your staff says one thing but the People say another?

Politician: I hire better people.

Director: Everyone on your team must be in tune with the People?

Politician: Yes. Otherwise we can't sing a very good song.

Director: General, is there any singing in your line of work?

Politician: Battle hymns, sure. And in yours?

Director: Not really. Some of those on my team like to sing but they mostly sing to themselves. The rest of the team likes it that way.

Politician: Who do you have to be in tune with? The customer?

Director: No, believe it or not.

Politician: Why not?

Director: We try to bring the customer into tune with us.

Politician: That's a good business to be in. You consult on making them more like you.

Director: Not exactly. We consult on bringing them more in line with themselves—making them the best they can be.

Politician: And the best harmonize with the best. And you're the best.

Director: We try.

General: But that's not true, the best harmonizing with the best. My best enemy in the field isn't in harmony with me. We clash.

Politician: Maybe there's a harmony you can't hear.

General: Maybe there is; maybe there isn't. But that's the difference between us, you know. My every effort is a striving toward this clash. I don't think you two have anything quite like it in your worlds.

6

Director: Which world has the most authority?

Politician: The political. We have civilian control of the military in this country, lest anyone forget.

General: True. But the business world controls the political world. Ha, ha.

Politician: It has an influence, but control is too strong a word. Government regulates business. You can't get around that fact.

Director: And the People control the government. Another fact?

General: What's wrong, Politician? You don't have anything to say?

Politician: I'm just marveling at the driving snow.

General: Oh, jokes about business aside—the People do control the government. Otherwise what's the point?

Politician: Otherwise why doesn't the military rule? Maybe you want to step in and restore the government to the People. But, it might take some time to do this—like a few decades. And by then? The military will have gotten efficient in rule. So....

General: Nonsense. As long as you chameleons have to be elected, and as long as elections are free, you're under control.

Director: Hmm. Are businesspeople part of the People?

Politician: Yes.

Director: So there's nothing wrong with business having some say over politicians.

General: Some say, sure. But it should be proportionate to their numbers.

Politician: I think it's fine for their money to play a role in politics—so long as they play by the rules.

General: But who makes the rules?

Director: General, you would defend these rules, wouldn't you?

General: Of course I would. With my life. But there's no harm in my offering a little criticism here and there.

Director: Agreed. And that's even though these rules have great authority.

Politician: These rules safeguard our freedom, our free election.

Director: And our way of life?

Politician: Of course.

Director: What is our way of life?

Politician: I can see you really are a philosopher

Director: On my good days, yes.

Politician: Well, you're in luck. I know what our way of life is as well as anyone. We believe in a dream.

Director: We believe in the dream or we live the dream?

Politician: You can believe and live at once.

Director: Okay. But what's the dream?

Politician: Opportunity.

Director: Opportunity to do what?

Politician: Get ahead.

Director: Get ahead of what?

General: The wolf.

Politician: The opportunity is to better our lives.

Director: Through money?

Politician: Yes, but other things, too.

Director: I'm glad to hear it. These other things can be very important in life. You bettered your life by winning your seat, right?

Politician: It's true.

Director: And that seat brings in not so much money, all things considered.

Politician: True.

Director: But you're happy, I suppose, with what you've got.

Politician: What are you getting at?

Director: The dream is about happiness.

Politician: You're only saying what everyone knows.

Director: So we're all justified in doing what makes us happy.

Politician: Within certain limits.

Director: What limits?

Politician: Your pursuit of happiness can't interfere with mine.

Director: I wouldn't dream of interfering with yours. But doesn't this interference happen all the time?

Politician: Of course it does. But there's something that needs to be said about the dream.

Director: What?

Politician: It's the highest authority in the land.

Director: The dream is the law of the land?

Politician: From which all other laws proceed. And yes, there's interference with the dream. But that doesn't mean the dream isn't valid.

Director: Valid?

Politician: True.

Director: The dream is true. But what does that mean?

Politician: There's no higher goal in life than happiness. And I am proud to serve the nation that looks to this as its guiding light.

7

Politician: No other nation has ever done this before.

Director: Other nations didn't want happiness?

Politician: Oh, they did. But they didn't devise a system to support it for as many as possible.

Director: That's the trick. How many can be happy? All of us?

Politician: No, not all of us. We have to be realistic. Some people wouldn't be happy if given a blank check on life.

Director: But certainly a majority.

Politician: That's the idea.

Director: No other nation has had its majority happy?

Politician: Maybe—but only by lucky chance. We have a science of politics behind us. That's why we're so successful.

Director: I thought we were so successful because of brave women and men.

Politician: We give those people a chance to thrive—by design. Bravery, with us, is allowed to shine.

Director: So it's not that we have more bravery than other nations in the past; it's that we put it to better use.

General: I don't think there's ever been a nation braver than ours.

Director: Not braver, but equally as brave?

General: Some of the Greeks were pretty tough. So were the Romans. The Brits. Hell, lots of people have been brave if you look across the centuries. But none of them were as smart about it as we are.

Director: Because of our technology?

General: No, and I hate hearing about how technology makes us the force we are. Give technology to a coward and watch him lose the fight. It all comes down to basics. Without them, technology means nothing.

Politician: So you'll ask for less money this year?

General: Bravery enhanced by technology is invincible. Of course, you have to have solid training. And very good leadership.

Director: And also a bit of luck?

General: I'd never turn down luck.

Director: So you build space into your plans for luck?

General: What? Of course not. Luck comes unbidden.

Politician: That's interesting about building space for luck. Our governmental system doesn't do that. It tries to harness Fortune; channel it; not let it have its way. But I'm not sure how good an idea that is.

Director: Why not?

Politician: Along with the lows we've clipped off some of the highs.

Director: Why can't we have the high without the low?

Politician: I don't know. There might be no good reason why.

Director: What do we mean by 'high'?

Politician: Unexpected good luck.

Director: Like finding a pot of gold?

Politician: Sure, but in leadership. That's a precious thing.

General: I have unexpected good luck all the time—in the good women and men who serve.

Director: But is it really luck? Don't we try to educate our citizens into becoming good women and men? Isn't that why we have success?

General: You need the right raw materials if you want your education to succeed.

Director: What are those raw materials, General?

General: A certain amount of intelligence and physical prowess. But there's something more, something that can't be explained. You just know it when you see it. That's the luck in this country. Finding these sorts of men.

Politician: And women.

General: Sure. But you know what I mean.

Director: And if the supply dries up, the country will collapse?

General: Not overnight. There's a certain momentum in things. But over time? Yes.

8

Director: What if the good men and women are gone for a while but then they come back?

General: There can be no gap. One generation is enough to finish the business.

Director: Who attains to authority in the gap?

General: There is no true authority in the gap. That's the problem.

Director: Who attains to false authority?

General: Charlatans. They seize authority every time.

Director: I've heard of seizing power. But authority?

General: With political power comes authority. If you deserve the power, your authority is true. If you don't, it's a lie—a sham. The important point, however, is that everything rides on each generation.

Politician: Of course. I can see this in the legislature. And I think we skipped our generation already. Today's generation is hardly what I'd call great.

Director: What are the men and women like?

Politician: Vain, unskilled, petty, treacherous—you name it.

Director: General, have you noticed this?

General: I'm afraid I have.

Director: So that's it? We're done?

General: Like I said, there's a certain momentum to things. We can carry on a while. How long, who can say? A lot of it comes down to luck. But the truth is—we're doomed.

Politician: And you're not even drunk.

General: Somehow I trust you two. Though if you ever repeat what I said, I'll deny having said it.

Director: Why?

General: A man in my position has to keep up a certain front, no matter what he really thinks. Can you lead troops into battle for a country you say is living on borrowed time?

Politician: Oh, but maybe we're wrong.

Director: How so?

Politician: In our country, each generation of conservatives sees the end of the world in the new generation. But this country keeps reinventing itself. That's why it goes on.

Director: So it won't be the end?

Politician: Of the world as we know it, yes it will. Of the country, no it won't.

Director: So if you stay focused on the country, can you reinvent yourself as appropriate?

Politician: Yes, but only for the right incentive.

Director: Authority?

Politician: To me authority is simply a tool.

Director: What do you want? Fame?

Politician: Fame is nice. But that's not it. I want to be happy.

Director: What would make you happy?

Politician: A major legislative win. I would take satisfaction in that.

Director: What legislation?

Politician: It doesn't matter. Just something big. You might be surprised how quickly I can become an expert on a topic, any topic.

Director: They teach you how to do that at law school, don't they? What's the trick?

Politician: There's a con to every pro, and a pro to every con.

General: With most things.

Politician: No, with everything. You learn all the pros, then you learn all the cons—and then you have a handle on all the angles. The rest is just filling in facts.

Director: Details. And you let your staff do that.

Politician: Right. It's not so hard.

Director: Then why isn't everyone as good at it as you?

Politician: People get hung up on the angles.

Director: What does that mean?

Politician: They really believe something is good or bad.

Director: You don't?

Politician: Of course I don't.

Director: Not even your own position?

Politician: Not even that. It's good because it's mine, of course. But I don't kid myself that it's somehow absolutely good.

Director: Any position that's yours is 'good'.

Politician: Correct.

Director: And that's why it's good.

Politician: That's right.

Director: You'd never pick a loser.

Politician: Never.

Director: So winners are good.

Politician: Winners are great.

Director: Then that's the trick. You know how to pick a winner.

Politician: Easy to say. Hard to do.

Director: What's so hard? You measure the forces in play and back the strongest.

Politician: Yes, Director. But like I said, people get hung up. They can't see things for what they are. This makes them hard to judge. If everyone were a rational player, it would be easy to know what to do.

Director: Are Congresspeople rational players?

Politician: Many are, believe it or not.

Director: How do you know they are?

Politician: In Congress we all face the same facts, more or less.

Director: Wait. Don't you all represent such different people?

Politician: Of course. But I'm talking about the facts of what it takes to pass a law. I know when a player is rational when they know what to do with the facts.

Director: Why wouldn't someone know what to do with the facts?

Politician: They get hung up on moral qualms.

Director: And you have none.

Politician: None.

Director: Are you saying you're amoral?

Politician: Oh, that sounds so harsh!

General: Are you?

Politician: Alright—yes. That's what allows me to see. And that, my friends, is the trick. But you won't see me raping and pillaging, and so on, and so on. I limit myself to things that serve my country best.

General: I don't like this at all. Especially since you oversee my soldiers and me!

Politician: Who would you rather had the job? Someone clear headed like me? Or someone shrouded in fog?

General: Director, say something here.

Director: I'm not sure Politician knows what morality is.

General: Tell him.

Director: Morality is a political thing.

Politician: Ha! Not what you wanted to hear, eh General?

General: Director, you have to explain.

Director: Politics is about how we live together. Our rules for living together are morals.

General: Yes, but Politician doesn't legislate morality. No one legislates morality.

Politician: You obviously haven't read your ancient history. Where do you think Spartan morals came from? Their lawgiver, Lycurgus.

General: Don't even think of comparing yourself to him.

Politician: I wouldn't dream it. But things are different in a democracy, which Sparta was emphatically not.

Director: How do they differ?

Politician: The People inform our every law.

General: As they should. And I'm sure they had a say in Sparta.

Politician: Not the say you would think. But we're not here to argue this.

General: No, we're not. We're more like Athens than Sparta. Athens was a democracy.

Politician: A democracy very different than ours. They had no real system of checks and balances. And the people got carried away. And, as I'm sure you know, they lost the great war to Sparta.

General: We're a sort of combination of the two.

Politician: Maybe. But we had many important influences from later times, too.

9

Director: Did we legislate these influences?

Politician: Some of them. But morals don't always come from laws.

General: Thank you for stating the obvious.

Director: Where do non-legislated morals come from?

Politician: From parents, friends, people you look up to. But it's best if they don't seem new. We generally want morals that are tested by time.

General: The best morals are handed down from one generation to the next, proven morals.

Director: Proven?

General: They breed success.

Director: So it's not morals for their own sake.

General: Who would want that?

Politician: Trust me, General. There's a crowd that does.

General: I could write a book called 'The Moral Foundation of Victory'.

Director: Why don't you?

General: Who has the time? Maybe when I retire some day.

Politician: If you write it now it might launch your career.

General: What career? My career is already launched.

Politician: Your political career.

General: Ha! Why would I want that?

Politician: Because it's more exciting than what you do now. Before you object, I know war can be very exciting. But for an upper level officer like you? You're on the receiving end of politics. Wouldn't you rather give?

General: Well, no doubt I receive. But give in what way?

Politician: A way that serves our forces well.

General: They could use some of that.

Politician: Then help yourself by helping them.

General: It's not about me.

Politician: No, of course not. It's about them. They're starved for true political leadership, General. You might be the one.

General: Oh, stop flattering me. Director, what do you make of this?

Director: Someone has to lead. Why not someone who knows the moral foundation of victory? That would amount to authority in its finest form. But....

General: But what?

Director: Who recognizes such authority? After all, authority only exists when it's recognized.

General: Everyone recognizes victory. Every single one.

Director: Sure, but do they always attribute it to its proper cause?

Politician: He has a point.

General: No doubt he does.

Director: So tell us, General. What morals lead to victory?

General: Above all else is perseverance.

Director: Why that?

General: Because—

Politician: Hold on. Is perseverance even a moral?

General: Try having any other moral without perseverance.

Politician: So it's the foundation of the foundation?

General: Yes.

Politician: What's the foundation of the foundation of the foundation?

General: I know you like to mock, but this is serious.

Director: I, in all seriousness, will say—the foundation Politician seeks is thought.

General: Why thought?

Director: We need to know what to persevere in. Thought leads us to knowledge, leads us to know. That's everything.

General: Well, that's obvious. I agree.

Politician: Yes, but what's the foundation of thought?

Director: It's in the nature of our soul.

Politician: So it's soul, thought, perseverance, morals, victory.

Director: Yes, but I would collapse soul and thought into one.

General: Why?

Director: Because thought is the activity of the soul.

General: So it's soul, perseverance, morals, victory.

Politician: I'd collapse it further. Soul, perseverance, victory.

General: I can live with that. In fact, I like it quite a bit! It's a good formula.

Politician: You could run for office on that.

General: Maybe I will. But seriously, I have a career. I can't see running for office any time soon.

Director: When you retire people will want you on their team—especially if you're known for Soul, Perseverance, and Victory.

Politician: People would consider you an authority on those things.

General: That's taking it a bit far. On victory maybe, and possibly perseverance. But who would claim to be an authority on soul?

Politician: I'm an authority on the soul of the People.

General: Because you win their votes?

Politician: Because I know what they need. That's why I win their votes.

Director: What do they need in their souls?

Politician: To feel they're a part of something greater than themselves.

General: It's the same in an army. Belonging is a need of the soul. When you belong you can persevere.

Director: You two are true authorities here. So tell me. Is it important to belong to something good? Or can you achieve the same effect if you belong to something bad?

General: Of course you have to belong to something good—great, even.

Politician: I don't think it's that simple. Something can feel good and actually be bad. But people still persevere.

Director: If it's bad why does it feel good?

General: Director is right. Bad never feels good. The real question is why people persevere in things that feel bad.

Politician: That's easy. It's because they think they're good.

Director: Why would they think that?

Politician: They take it on authority.

Director: Whose authority?

Politician: Everyone has their own authority they look to. Sometimes the authority is good; sometimes the authority is bad.

Director: What makes an authority good?

General: Perseverance and soul.

Director: Not victory?

General: If it takes victory in order for an authority to be good, we have a problem.

Politician: What problem?

General: The bad can win. And then we need resistance.

Director: And there are authorities in the resistance.

General: Yes, of course. But they've yet to win. Does that mean they're no good?

Director: I see your point. But here's what I wonder. Perseverance and soul no doubt can help, but they're no guarantee of victory.

General: Yes, that's true. Victory does depend on other things, too.

Director: What other things?

General: The things to do with force.

Director: Does force make for authority?

General: Force alone? That makes for bad authority.

Director: What else do we need in order to have good authority?

Politician: Reason, the action of soul.

Director: General?

General: Force and reason can make for authority.

Director: True authority?

General: Yes.

Politician: What about reason alone? Authority?

General: Director, you should answer this.

Director: I'm inclined to say reason is without authority.

Politician: But that's nonsense. Courts reason and their reasoning has great authority.

Director: You may think I'm quibbling, but courts use legal reasoning, not natural reasoning.

General: What's natural reasoning?

Director: Reasoning not backed by authority.

General: Why not make use of authority if you can?

Director: Authority interferes with reason.

Politician: It's that simple?

Director: In some ways? Yes.

General: But why?

Director: It has to do with what authority is.

General: What is authority?

Director: Authority is something that commands.

General: And reason cannot be commanded.

Director: Not to any good end. Reason needs free play.

General: Politician, what do you think of that?

Politician: It's true. But, unfortunately, sometimes reason is only that.

General: Only what?

Politician: Play.

Director: Why do you say that?

Politician: While reason has a force of its own, not everyone feels it. With them reason has no bite. And so it's only play.

10

Director: Why do you think people don't feel the force of reason?

Politician: You want us to say authority gets in the way.

General: That can't be the only reason.

Director: What other reason is there?

General: Some people are just born that way.

Politician: I completely disagree. Everyone is born to reason. Director?

Director: I don't know for sure, but I'm inclined to say uninhibited humans are born to reason.

General: Are you saying some people are inhibited as soon as they're born?

Director: Yes. It's very bad luck.

General: And it's always by authority?

Director: There might be other reasons. But authority is clearly one.

General: Abusive authority.

Director: Yes.

Politician: What's the opposite of abusive authority?

Director: Guiding authority—that helps a tree grow straight and tall.

General: What does the tree stand for?

Director: The soul.

Politician: Director, what did you say is the action of the soul?

Director: Reason.

Politician: Does reason need something to help it grow?

Director: It needs resistance so it grows strong.

Politician: But not too much resistance?

Director: How much is too much depends on the strength of the soul. Souls are born with different strengths.

General: What makes for strength of soul?

Politician: I thought you were the authority here.

General: What's the answer, Director?

Director: Maybe science will tell us soon.

General: No, this isn't something for science to say. Science can't know everything.

Director: And yet science is in some ways the greatest authority of our age.

General: For some.

Director: What competing authorities are there? Politicians?

General: Ha! Not even Politician thinks that.

Politician: I can tell you the authority many of my constituents look to—God.

Director: Do you look to that authority, Politician?

Politician: I look to myself. And you, General?

General: I mostly look to myself, as well. You, Director?

Director: We three have something in common. But I have something more.

General: What?

Director: Reason.

Politician: Reason is your authority? I thought reason and authority don't get along.

Director: Reason is what I look to beyond looking to myself.

Politician: I thought reason comes from within.

General: Politician, there are things within that are from beyond.

Politician: The Great Beyond, General?

General: Why not?

Politician: Director, do you agree with that? That there are things within from beyond?

Director: Oh, I certainly do. But by 'beyond' I just mean outside ourselves.

Politician: Other people.

Director: Yes.

Politician: So we have to eject these things we have in us from other people.

Director: Often times, yes. But not always.

Politician: When wouldn't we?

Director: When these things stand to reason.

Politician: Because they came from reasonable people?

Director: We can say that.

Politician: Why do you hedge?

Director: We haven't discussed what it means to be reasonable. One type of 'reasonable' should be looked to. The other should not.

Politician: And that which we look to is, or becomes, authority.

Director: Yes.

Politician: So what's the type of 'reasonable' we should look to?

Director: The kind like you.

General: Oh, be serious.

Politician: I think he is.

Director: I am.

Politician: What's good about me?

Director: While you're flexible, you arrive at a reasoned conclusion and hold fast.

General: How do you know that?

Director: He's on television a lot.

Politician: How do you know others don't tell me what to conclude?

Director: It wouldn't matter if they did.

Politician: Did you hear that, General? It doesn't matter if we think for ourselves!

Director: You have to think in the sense of weighing and considering what you hear.

General: Of course you do. I have a staff I listen to. Every good leader does.

Politician: Is your staff your authority?

General: Often times, yes. I look to them.

Politician: And yet you always have authority over them. A different kind of authority.

General: As do you over your staff. But we also have the other sort of authority, the sort our staffs have. If we didn't, we never would have been given the authority of position or title.

Politician: Don't be so sure.

Director: If you could only have one type of authority, which would it be?

General: The one truly worth having—that of knowledge or wisdom.

Politician: Position without wisdom is worse than useless. But I think there's a difference between knowledge and wisdom.

Director: What's the difference?

Politician: You can know without being wise.

Director: Can you be wise without knowing?

Politician: You can be 'wise', yes. But not truly wise.

Director: How do you get a reputation for wisdom without being wise?

Politician: You tell people what they want to hear.

Director: That's what politicians do.

Politician: Not all of them. Or at least not all the time.

Director: If you don't tell people what they want to hear, how do you get elected?

Politician: By showing them you're wise enough to successfully navigate most situations.

Director: Yes, but what situations? Electoral debates?

Politician: You show that at each step along the way in your career you met with success. That builds confidence. Confidence translates into votes.

Director: People like a winner.

Politician: Exactly.

Director: And if you're always winning either you know something or you're very lucky.

Politician: Both good things as far as voters are concerned.

Director: If voters had to choose between knowledge and luck, which would it be?

Politician: Luck, every time.

Director: General?

General: I'd rather be lucky than good.

Director: But isn't it good to be good?

General: Of course. But good without luck often ends up... bad.

11

Director: So when you make military plans, you should account for luck.

General: It's next to impossible to account for luck. At best you can build in a margin of error.

Director: Why not call it a margin of luck?

General: Ha, ha. Since luck can turn the tides of war, that sounds like good advice.

Politician: Tell us, Director. Does philosophy account for luck?

Director: Philosophy wants to make room for luck.

Politician: Why?

Director: Because luck can produce the unexpected.

Politician: And that's important to philosophy?

Director: It is.

Politician: Why?

Director: It gives us room to breathe.

Politician: When it doesn't choke us. I leave as little to luck as possible.

Director: You don't trust your luck?

Politician: I don't trust my grandmother. Why should I trust my luck?

General: You really don't need luck in your campaigns?

Politician: Who can't do with a little good luck? But there's no luck in figuring out what the People want. And that's the key. The best politicians lead through what they want.

General: 'They' being the majority.

Politician: Of course.

General: And what about the few, the proud who stand aside from the rest?

Politician: Bad luck for them. Oh, I'm just kidding! I certainly do what I can for them, as well. But it's funny to hear a uniformed officer talking about those who stand aside.

General: Rooks can stand aside on the board. And yet they're one with the pawns. They serve the same end.

Director: The king's. Who is our king?

Politician: The People are king.

Director: Who is the People's queen?

Politician: That's a good question.

General: Who, Director?

Director: Philosophy.

Politician: Ha!

Director: Why do you laugh?

Politician: Philosophy wants nothing to do with the People.

Director: Why do you say that?

Politician: Philosophy wants you to think. Every politician knows the people don't want to think.

Director: Do you think?

Politician: I think.

Director: Do you want to think?

Politician: I always do what I want.

Director: If you think, why don't you want people to think?

Politician: It's not up to me what they want or don't. I simply take them as I find them. And I find they, generally, don't want to think.

Director: So you do the thinking for them?

Politician: Yes. And if they like what I think, I win. Simple.

Director: What do you think?

Politician: Winning thoughts, Director. Watch me on television some day and you'll see very well what I think.

Director: I have. But I can't get away from a sneaking suspicion.

Politician: What suspicion?

Director: You say you always do what you want.

Politician: Yes?

Director: Do you want to say what you say on television?

Politician: I do. So I can win.

Director: Winning, yes. But do you always believe what you say?

Politician: It's not about belief.

Director: It's about winning, yes. You want to win, and so everything you do toward that end is something you want to do.

Politician: I'm glad you understand so well.

Director: So am I. But let's suppose winning requires you to paint a yellow stripe down your back. Is that something you want to do?

General: Ha!

Politician: I'm glad you're having fun at my expense, philosopher. But I'll answer your question, the broader question. No, not everything I must do, do I want to do.

Director: Why not?

Politician: Do you like living in a clean house?

Director: I do.

Politician: Do you like to clean?

Director: No, not especially.

Politician: And yet you do it?

Director: I do.

Politician: Because the end requires the means?

Director: The end requires its means.

Politician: Well then, think of my campaigns as great national house cleanings.

General: He's pretty good, Director.

Director: Yes, General, he is. But I want him to be better.

Politician: How?

Director: General, do you see? He really wants to know.

General: I believe he does. So how can he be better?

Director: He can focus more.

Politician: Focus? I'm more focused than any politician I know!

Director: Yes, but what's that you're wearing?

Politician: What, this? It's a watch, Director.

Director: Yes, but how much did it cost?

Politician: More than I care to say.

Director: Why not say? Not very popular to be wearing a watch like that? Here, switch it with mine.

Politician: What, that plastic piece of junk? No thanks.

General: I've known some foreign tyrants who wear watches like Politician's. Quite impressive.

Director: Why do you think they wear them?

General: To enhance their authority.

Director: Authority can be bought?

General: Let's just say it can be enhanced.

Director: Then my apologies, Politician. I wasn't aware you were enhancing your authority. A worthy cause.

Politician: The funny thing is, Director, I can't tell if you're being serious or sarcastic.

Director: Serious. I think you're a good politician. If this watch earns you respect, or whatever, then I'm in favor of it. You see, I want you to come to power— more power than you have now.

Politician: Why?

Director: Because you're flexible and... plausible.

General: Ha, ha! Plausible!

Politician: Credible, is what he meant to say.

Director: Maybe so. However that may be, I think you'd be good for us all. You could accomplish significant things. Isn't that what you want?

Politician: You know it's what I want.

Director: You need authority to do it. Yes, you need to keep winning office. But you need to go beyond that. Not everyone in office has authority.

Politician: That's very true.

General: Director, say more about this.

Director: What gives someone authority?

General: People's desire to look to them.

Director: Well, what if the one with authority has to do things that would cause people to look away?

General: What kind of things?

Director: Necessary things.

General: Necessary for what?

Director: The success of the cause. Do I need to explain what the cause is?

General: No. In the end, I serve the cause. But if you're serving the cause, why would they look away?

Director: Does everyone serve the cause?

General: No, certainly not everyone.

Director: Those who don't serve might not like what they see. Does that make sense?

General: It does.

Politician: Yes, but I need to know—what is the cause?

Director: You really don't know? The cause is the cause of philosophy.

12

General: Director, I don't serve the cause of philosophy.

Director: But, General, I think you do.

General: What is the cause of philosophy?

Director: Unbridled thought.

General: I'm in favor of that.

Politician: As am I.

Director: Then we three agree. So tell me. What bridles thought?

Politician: Wars.

General: Elections.

Director: Why?

Politician: You need to pull everyone together.

Director: Are you saying you bridle your own thought, or that of those who follow you?

Politician: That of those who follow you.

Director: Do all leaders do this?

Politician: Of course—the good ones, at least.

Director: So it matters who's in power.

Politician: That goes without saying.

Director: What kind of person should be in power?

Politician: What kind? Me.

Director: Because you know how to pull people together?

Politician: That's right. But also because I'm flexible and I have lots of experience.

Director: Is there any other reason?

General: He has a keen mind.

Director: Agreed.

Politician: Thank you. But is that all you two can say? What about my integrity?

Director: Don't brag about things you haven't got.

Politician: Are you serious? Do you know how many opportunities I've had to take what isn't mine?

General: Oh, he's just teasing, Politician. We all know you're true.

Politician: Tell me, Director. Does General have integrity?

Director: Yes.

Politician: Well then, you're going to have to tell me more. What is integrity?

Director: When you put your money where your mouth is.

Politician: Ha! Look at him smirk!

General: Seriously, Director. How do you define integrity?

Director: Having principles you live by.

Politician: I have principles I live by.

Director: In your political life, yes. But General doesn't distinguish between his military life and some other life. His life is one. I don't think yours is. That's why I say you haven't got integrity.

Politician: Do you think I should live one life, as you say?

Director: All I can do is tell you that I live one life, the life of philosophy. General and I have much in common.

Politician: Does this 'one life' make you more of an authority?

Director: I don't know. I suppose it's possible.

General: Oh, don't be shy, Director. Of course it makes you more of an authority. People can sense integrity, or oneness of life.

Director: Well, there it is, Politician. Maybe you should get some more oneness in your life.

Politician: My life is going just fine, thanks. Except for being stuck here in this blizzard.

Director: It's not so bad, is it? We have warmth, drink, pleasant and comfortable surroundings.

Politician: Can something be pleasant but not comfortable?

Director: See, General? He's a real thinker. That's what I like about him.

Politician: See how he dodged the question, General? I see a politician in him.

General: You two should trade places for a week.

Politician: Government would grind to a halt from endless debate!

Director: Philosophy would be ashamed to show its face for all the lies!

General: Seriously, now. Can politicians be philosophers?

Politician: Why not? A Roman emperor was once a philosopher.

Director: At best he was a politician first and some sort of 'philosopher' second.

General: What about philosophers as politicians?

Director: I think it's possible.

Politician: But as a philosopher first and some sort of 'politician' second.

Director: Yes. And now that you mention it, that's what I think you should be.

13

Politician: What would it mean to be a philosopher first?

Director: You shed your authority.

Politician: How can I govern without authority?

Director: You have to persuade by other means. You have to work harder.

Politician: But philosophers reason, and reason surely has authority.

Director: Reason has no authority. You either listen to it or you don't.

General: But we look to reason.

Director: We look to the stars to navigate at night. That doesn't mean the stars are authorities. The stars just are, and we look to them in order to know where we are.

Politician: And reasons 'just are'?

Director: Reasons just are.

General: But if a philosopher gains a reputation for always following reason, won't that philosopher become an authority in the eyes of many?

Director: Perhaps, but it's undeserved.

Politician: Why?

Director: Those many can just as easily follow reason themselves.

General: It's not always easy to follow reason, to put it mildly. So when someone does manage to do it, I'd say they deserve to be an authority to those who would follow reason.

Director: Hmm. That makes me wonder.

General: About what?

Director: Regardless of who is or isn't an authority, authority itself—what does it stand in contrast with?

General: Lack of authority.

Director: Is there a word for lack of authority?

General: I'm not sure there is.

Director: That's a curious thing. It's as if lack of authority doesn't exist.

General: We should give it a name.

Politician: Neutrality.

Director: Why that?

Politician: Because when you're an authority on an issue, you generally find yourself on a side.

Director: But if you have no authority, you can afford to be neutral?

General: I like the idea of neutrality. Soldiers are neutral when it comes to political things. How is it with philosophy?

Director: Philosophy questions no matter who is in charge. So, again, it seems we have much in common.

Politician: You have less in common with General than you let on.

Director: And more in common with you?

Politician: Yes. Especially if I lead from a position of no authority.

General: You seem taken with that idea.

Politician: It's liberating. I don't much like being an authority. I want to lead from natural persuasion.

General: I don't have that luxury. The entire military is based on authority.

Politician: Then maintain your authority however you must—but persuade. Persuasive authority is the greatest authority there can be.

Director: Persuasion without authority is the greatest persuasion there can be.

Politician: If that's true, General needs to let down his authority now and then.

General: That's rarely possible for me—and it might backfire.

Politician: How so?

General: I think you can imagine how so.

Politician: I hope you're not being defensive in this. We must always be on offense. If authority is defensive, I want nothing to do with it.

Director: But isn't it inherently defensive?

Politician: What, it's a shield and not a spear?

General: What's the spear?

Politician: Reason.

General: Director, do you believe that?

Director: I'm not sure I like military metaphors here. Reason is a way of coming to see.

Politician: What good is sight?

Director: I see you have some philosopher blood. But do you want the blind to steer the ship of state?

Politician: No, of course not. So leaders must see, but see without authority?

Director: That sounds about right.

General: But if they have no authority, who will care what they see?

Director: You must patiently explain what you see, over and over again.

General: Yes, but there are urgent times, times when there's no time to explain again and again.

Politician: That's when you're forced to lean on your authority.

Director: So we need to keep authority in reserve, for emergencies?

Politician: Of course.

Director: How do we stockpile authority?

Politician: Oh, you can't store it up. You need to maintain it along the way. And that's a dilemma for me—as you'd have me, Director.

Director: Yes, Politician, it is. But are we really saying reason isn't exactly what's needed for urgent times?

Politician: Maybe it is. So long as it's backed by personality.

General: The cult of personality.

Politician: Call it whatever you will. Personality is different than authority.

Director: How?

Politician: People are compelled to follow authority. But people want to follow, positively want to follow—personality.

Director: Why do you think that is?

Politician: Who knows why? All I know is that personality is sweeter than authority.

Director: What is personality?

Politician: It's the human shining through.

Director: Maybe the human is the ultimate authority?

Politician: No, I don't think so. Authority compels. The human persuades. You won't get me to change my mind on this.

Director: And persuasion is always better than compulsion.

Politician: Always, if it can be helped.

General: Since it can't always be helped, we do need a reserve of authority.

Politician: Some people simply won't allow themselves to be persuaded. So, yes.

Director: What if you yourself are without authority, but you surround yourself with those who have it?

General: That's a situation ripe for a coup!

Director: Let's say you persuade those around you. They simply back up what you say.

Politician: I think that's how it has to be. No coup, and they help you get what you want.

14

Director: You get what you want because, in part, authority has force. No?

Politician: Yes.

Director: Why does authority have force?

Politician: Habit, for one.

Director: Can you say more?

Politician: People get in the habit of looking to authority. Habits are hard to break.

Director: Is habit a good reason to follow authority?

Politician: I don't know if it's good. But I know it happens.

Director: Can you live with that?

Politician: I already do.

Director: Well, philosophers don't want this habit.

Politician: What kind of habit do they want?

Director: They don't want any kind of habit, except perhaps the habit of giving reason a chance.

Politician: Being open to persuasion. But so few people are.

Director: What gets in the way?

Politician: Emotion.

Director: What kind of emotion?

Politician: Anger, fear, jealousy—you name it.

General: Director, do philosophers have these emotions under control?

Director: As far as they are philosophers? They don't even feel them.

Politician: Philosophers have no feeling at all? Is that what you're saying?

Director: No, but philosophers in the act of philosophizing know there's nothing to be angry about, nothing to fear, and nothing to be jealous of.

Politician: I don't believe you.

Director: Then let me tell you what philosophers do feel. Philosophers feel excitement, disappointment, hatred, and love.

Politician: Oh, you're just making all of this up. Why can't you feel anger if you feel hatred?

General: I'll answer, Director. Hatred is cold. Anger is hot.

Politician: You can have cold anger, at least I can. And are disappointment and fear all that far apart?

General: Of course they are! Who's making things up now? The important thing is that Director said philosophers can feel love.

Politician: Yes, that's a very good point, General. Love is the key to all the other emotions. So if he admits that, he admits them all.

Director: Fair enough. And I do feel love—more often than not, in fact. I'm something of an authority on love.

Politician: We're all authorities on our own love.

Director: If so, if we could tap into that, we'd all be more open to persuasion and less in need of other kinds of authority.

Politician: Do you really believe those in love are open to persuasion? It seems the opposite to me.

Director: Oh, they're not open concerning their love. But to other things? I think they often are.

General: I think Director has a point. Those in love can be generous, and so on, to everyone else.

Politician: Except when they're love sick.

Director: Yes, but either way these lovers pose a challenge to you.

Politician: Oh? How so?

Director: They listen to their beloved more than you.

Politician: Of course they do! General, I think Director has had one too many drinks. Let's cut him off and send him to bed!

General: But he does have a certain point.

Politician: Oh, no! Not you, too.

General: Reason should persuade, whatever the source. If the beloved speaks reason, more power to them. If not, more power to you. But reason must win.

Director: You have to make yourself more attractive than all the beloveds in the land.

Politician: You really are crazy, you know? And how do I do that?

Director: You strip yourself of authority. If the beloveds did that, things would be infinitely better for us all.

Politician: You think beloveds revel in their authority, the authority of love?

Director: Many of them do, yes. For some, it's their only real taste of power. That's hard to let go.

Politician: So how do I overcome that?

Director: You appeal to the lovers' pride.

Politician: They take pride in being persuaded by me?

Director: They take pride in joining reason's side. And if their beloved comes along, that's great. If not, it opens up a certain distance.

Politician: Listen to Director. He wants me to get in between a lover and their beloved.

Director: Only if the beloved isn't open to reason. Otherwise, things are fine.

Politician: This is dangerous stuff.

General: Welcome to the club. I deal in dangerous stuff every day.

Politician: And you, Director. What danger for you?

Director: You two could turn on me. And then I have two very dangerous enemies.

Politician: Oh, we're not going to turn on you. This is one of the more entertaining conversations I've had in a while. General?

General: On my honor, I won't turn.

Politician: Why are you so serious?

General: Because we're talking about serious things.

Politician: We're talking about authority. That's not so serious, is it?

General: Try leading an army without it.

15

General: But my interest is in more than that. Director, one day when I retire, I too, will be a civilian. So tell me. If you have to have authority in the civilian world, how best should you have it?

Director: As lightly as possible.

Politician: But with crushing force as needed, to protect it.

General: But tyrants use force to protect their authority.

Director: What do they love about authority that they'd protect it so?

Politician: It gets them what they want.

Director: What do they want?

Politician: To be admired. To be loved.

Director: So tyrants think these things can be forced. Can they?

General: Of course not.

Politician: Well....

General: Well what?

Politician: Among a certain crowd, they can.

Director: Why?

Politician: Because certain people worship force. Force is the ultimate authority for them. Sorry to say it, Director, but philosophy stands no chance.

Director: And politicians do?

Politician: Law does. The force of the law—backed by troops.

Director: Can we simply replace the authority of force with law?

Politician: In our land? We already have. This is a nation of laws.

Director: But we have to be careful.

Politician: Why?

Director: Law can't reason.

Politician: What's that supposed to mean?

Director: The statue of Justice is blind. Should our highest authority be blind?

General: Our justice isn't perfect, Director. No doubt. But until we know how to improve it, we leave it as it is.

Politician: Yes, General. But what's wrong with Justice being blind? Her scales are impartial and weigh quite well.

Director: Nothing is wrong—so long as you don't mind Her always choosing a pound of rocks over an ounce of gold.

Politician: Well, I know how to fix that.

General: How?

Politician: Put me in charge.

General: Ha! Director, have you ever met such a confident man?

Director: A few times, yes. But none with so much promise.

General: Promise to supercede Justice?

Politician: Oh, I'd work within the law. I'd only make the law better. Leave us with more room to breathe.

General: What's that supposed to mean?

Politician: Leave more room for interpretation. Wouldn't you like more leeway in your command?

General: I would.

Politician: That's the kind of thing I'm talking about. And Director, that increases the role of philosophy.

Director: Because people will use reason to interpret? They'll look before they leap?

Politician: Precisely.

Director: But that's what lawyers are for. Your program only increases their power.

Politician: Lawyers and philosophers have much in common.

Director: Oh? What do they have in common?

Politician: A love of words.

Director: Lawyers love the authority of words.

Politician: They love the ambiguity of words.

General: Which is just what gives them power! Ambiguity makes them needed, makes them valued, gives them authority. Law should be a simple thing that everyone can understand, not the complex province of an elite.

Politician: Sounds like General is ready to run for office.

General: I'll never run.

Politician: Maybe. But politics is in your future. And I'm an authority here.

16

General: Why shouldn't I just retire when I retire?

Politician: Because you have the itch.

General: What itch?

Politician: The itch to be an authority.

Director: It's not an itch for power?

Politician: Some people love power; some people love authority. Our good General here loves having authority—even if not command.

Director: What is it about authority that's so appealing to some people?

Politician: They love having people look to them, especially in a crisis. It makes them feel important, special, needed. Don't get me wrong, I love having authority, too.

Director: I thought we were going to strip you of that and leave persuasion.

Politician: If you're persuasive often enough, you become an authority on those things. There's no way around it.

Director: Then my hopes for you are dashed.

Politician: General, is he being serious or sarcastic?

General: I can't tell. Maybe ironic?

Politician: I think Director loves authority, in his way—the authority of philosophy.

Director: That's exactly what I don't love. Philosophy shouldn't have authority.

General: Why not?

Director: Because it wants others to look to themselves, especially in times of crisis.

Politician: Then philosophy is dangerous.

General: How so?

Politician: Imagine if all your troops looked to themselves in a time of crisis—and not to you.

General: Dangerous, yes. But that's not what philosophy does, right Director?

Director: Yes and no.

General: How so?

Director: Yes, it seeks to encourage people to look to themselves. But it also seeks to encourage them to look to others.

General: What are they looking for? Truth?

Director: Yes, truth. But also ideas, beliefs.

Politician: What do they do when they find them? See if one suits the situation at hand?

Director: That's what often happens. And I don't think it takes a great amount of skill. So anyone can do it. No, the difficult thing is to disabuse people of ideas that are doing them harm, ideas that harm the cause.

Politician: It's harder to persuade someone out of something than into it. I agree. I like to think of that as my strength. I want to be known as the Great Dissuader.

Director: Ah, my hopes for you are rising.

Politician: I'll dissuade them of everything, leaving them only the one true cause—whatever that cause might be! Ha, ha!

General: Oh, don't laugh about that.

Politician: Sometimes it's good to laugh at the things we take seriously.

Director: General, what is the cause?

General: The strength and welfare of the Republic.

Director: Politician, and I'm asking you seriously now—can you promise to serve that cause?

Politician: I can. And you, Director?

Director: Yes, but I have to qualify what General said. The cause is the strength and welfare of the true Republic.

Politician: Yes.

General: I agree with that.

Director: Interesting, I thought one of you might object. What's a false republic?

General: One example is when a group of people seizes power and manipulates things at the expense of others. That's not the true Republic. The true Republic isn't capable of that.

Politician: Yes, and the true Republic doesn't launch cynical wars, and so on.

Director: Is the true Republic just?

General: Absolutely.

Politician: If politics isn't about justice, what's it about? Do you know what I mean?

Director: Yes, I think I understand. You want to be known as a believer in justice. But what are we saying? We should all be authorities on the true Republic?

General: That's what it means to be a Citizen.

Director: Authority is woven into the fabric of our political life.

General: The authority of the individual citizen flies in our flag.

Director: But we're distinguishing authority from power.

General: Well, yes.

Director: Politician?

Politician: Look at that snow. Oh, did you say something, Director? Power? Yes, not everyone can have power. The elected have power. That's how the Republic works.

Director: But we all have authority?

Politician: It's true. Citizens have the authority to elect. And that's the highest authority in the land. The elected can have authority, but it never goes beyond the basic, fundamental authority of the Citizen.

17

Director: But why not call what the Citizens have 'power', not 'authority'. They have the power to elect.

Politician: Words, words, words. I love it. But it doesn't matter here either way. Call it power if you like.

Director: But are power and authority really interchangeable?

General: Of course not. You can have power and no authority.

Politician: Oh, I don't believe it. Give an example.

General: I might have the power to attack the enemy, but no authority to do so.

Director: That seems like a fine example to me.

Politician: Alright. But that authority comes from people like me.

Director: Authority, not power, right? I mean, you don't have the power to attack. You have the authority to let loose those with the power.

Politician: I think you're splitting hairs.

General: No, I think it's an important distinction, Politician. Without me, you have no power to attack. Without you, I have no authority to attack. I've met arrogant politicians who don't seem to understand this. They think they have all the power.

Director: Well, Politician?

Politician: Since it doesn't really matter, I'll say I agree with all that.

Director: That kind of attitude won't get you very far.

Politician: I've come pretty far already.

Director: But you want to go further. We're trying to equip you with what you need.

Politician: What equipment do I need?

General: You need to understand that people hate arrogance.

Politician: True. They love flair, in a winner. What else do I need to understand?

General: People need to know you're on their team.

Politician: I'm the quarterback. Of course I'm on the team.

Director: Would you rather be the coach?

Politician: Coaching suits you better than me. I'm a player.

General: And what am I?

Politician: Oh, you're a player, too. But you're on defense. So tell me, Coach, what's the next play?

Director: One where you give the ball to someone else.

Politician: That's what quarterbacks do. But what's the ball?

Director: The glory.

General: Ha, ha. Don't be a glory boy, friend.

Politician: But the better I do, the better does the team.

Director: What's the team?

Politician: The country. What else?

Director: What's good for you is good for the country?

Politician: Yes.

Director: He smiles. But it's a smile that suggests he knows he's right!

General: Could he be right?

Director: It's hard to say. He'd have to be really, really good at what he does.

Politician: I am. Making the country good makes me look good, and I'm all about looking good.

General: There's nothing untrue in that.

Director: No, I dare say there isn't. But I have a doubt.

Politician: I'll dispel it.

Director: What makes the country good?

General: Yes, that's the thing. Well, Politician?

18

Politician: The country is good when everyone works together well.

Director: Toward some common end?

Politician: No, not necessarily. There can be many ends. You have your end; I have mine. That's the beauty. We can work together and help serve each other's end. Figuring out who works well together is half the battle. I'm very good at this.

Director: How did you become so good at it?

Politician: Ever since I was a young boy I found ways to make peace through clever combinations.

Director: Peace? Or harmony?

Politician: Harmony is the better word. Thank you, Coach.

Director: But not everyone harmonizes, no matter how good you are.

Politician: Correct. That's when I bring in others and shake things up. Harmony eventually happens.

Director: Because those who don't harmonize leave?

Politician: Yes. They go off and find their musical mates.

Director: And this conducting was your first taste of authority?

Politician: That's right. People looked to me from then until now.

Director: But surely other people do this sort of thing all the time. General, don't you have staff conflicts you have to resolve?

General: Certainly.

Politician: Resolve them into harmony, or just resolve? Be honest.

General: You have a point. We don't always find harmony.

Director: I think what Politician is talking about is difficult. I think the secret is allowing for multiple ends.

General: Yes, but what about the cause?

Politician: Here's the thing. Not everyone is meant to serve the cause.

General: They're not meant to, or they simply don't?

Politician: They're not meant to. It can't be helped.

Director: Why not?

Politician: You know why not. Suffice it to say, my goal is to find all those who are meant to serve, and get them into a place where they can.

Director: What is this, some sort of elite?

Politician: It is what it is. But elite or not doesn't really matter. When you're doing what you love, you don't care about that. In fact, if I get the sense someone cares about status I move them on to somewhere else.

Director: You're more of a coach than I.

Politician: I'm a player-coach, yes. And I need my harmony, too.

General: But what you're suggesting, taken on a large scale, requires a great deal of power.

Politician: Don't you think I should have it?

General: You need the proper authority first.

Politician: Yes, we need to change the rules to suit my skills.

General: Director, do you think he's crazy?

Director: Not if Politician really can do what he says. But this might require a fundamental amendment.

Politician: If that's what it takes, that's what it takes. I want this all to be legit, under the proper authority.

General: You want the authorities to grant you authority.

Politician: Yes. I'll take care of the power myself.

Director: What authority would you seek, anyway?

Politician: I want to be Speaker of the House.

Director: Is that all?

Politician: Well, I do want to expand the power of the Speaker. I want the Speaker to appoint one of the Senators from each state.

General: Ha!

Politician: But there's more. I want these Senators to serve at the pleasure of the House.

General: You think people will vote for that?

Politician: Stranger things have happened.

Director: Why do you think people would like this idea?

Politician: The House is generally more answerable to the people. The House is more in touch.

Director: And democracy is all about being in touch.

Politician: Yes, essentially.

General: Am I missing something or are you making it less of a democracy by taking the vote for the Senator away from the People? Besides, the People don't choose the Speaker. The House majority members do.

Politician: Details. The point is that with me in place as Speaker, I can get the right people in the right places and have... harmony. But don't get me wrong. I'm not wed to this idea. There are other ways to go. This one just seems easiest to me.

General: Easy? I'd hate to think what you think would be hard!

Director: Yes, if you can get the votes, Politician, I think you might do much good. But what about those who come after you? Isn't there much risk of harm? Or will you be in a position to keep things under control?

Politician: What position do you have in mind?

Director: Would you run for President?

Politician: No. That job is no fun.

General: And the Speakership is?

Politician: Of course it is! You can do a lot more. People don't scrutinize you as much.

Director: You can fly under the radar?

Politician: Compared to the President? Yes, of course. Besides, the President can't make laws. Laws are what this country is all about. Speakers make laws. That's what I want. Laws to free the people and reign the President in.

General: The President would never sign such things into law—reigning in, that is.

Politician: With the Senate under control and the House in my hands? The President would have no choice.

Director: What would be your major legislative push?

Politician: Healthcare reform.

General: Why that?

Politician: Everyone cares about health. Health is the most important thing. Health is the promise of the scientific revolution. Without health, all of our discoveries are for nothing.

Director: Do you have any ideas about what laws you'd pass?

Politician: I'd need to see the new lay of the land before I could say for sure. But I will say that everyone should be insured along the lines of Social Security.

General: Ha! That's hardly the model of success.

Politician: And yet millions of people do well by it.

General: But the money is running out.

Politician: And that's where the similarity ends. We're going to drive down the costs of healthcare.

General: How? Medicine is expensive.

Politician: People shouldn't go into medical fields because of money. My prime example is the veterinarian field. These people work, for much less money than their human services peers, tirelessly out of love. I want those in the human medical endeavor to work tirelessly out love, as well.

General: CEOs of giant pharmaceutical corporations should work tirelessly out of love?

Politician: Yes. And if they don't? They're not making much harmony here.

Director: You would have them removed?

Politician: Removed and replaced by love.

General: People will learn to fake love.

Politician: That's why you need those who know true love when they see it.

Director: It takes one to know one?

Politician: Yes, and that's why I need to stack the Senate with those who love.

Director: Love, not skill, is your criterion?

Politician: Love that serves itself with skill is my criterion.

Director: How do you serve yourself?

Politician: How do you, Director, serve yourself?

Director: I make sure my thinking is clear. Will your Senators' thoughts be clear, or mushy in love?

Politician: Mushy. Ha, ha. No, I'm not bringing on sentimentalists. I want deep and powerful love, love for the Republic and all its Citizens. This love wants it and them to be well.

General: Will this mean higher taxes?

Politician: Yes, but only up to the amount of what the Citizens already pay for health.

Director: They're simply transferring the money to you.

Politician: To be put to better use, yes.

General: So Citizens will pay the same amount but get better care?

Politician: Exactly. A win-win if you ask me.

Director: Certainly that's a win-win. But what about the entire medical industry? They're a major lobbying force.

Politician: Senators and those in the House will owe more to me than them.

Director: So the lobbyists get squeezed out.

Politician: Yes. But there are those who will jump to fill their shoes, even for much less money.

Director: Idealists?

Politician: And hard headed scientists, too.

General: You really think you can curb the urge to get rich?

Politician: I do. I'll replace it—with love for honor and fame.

19

Director: What do others say when you tell them all this?

Politician: This is the first time I've spoken it aloud. So what do you say?

General: I say it's crazy enough it just might work.

Politician: And you, Director?

Director: Honor-and-fame is good for some. But don't you think there will always be those motivated by money? What do you do with them?

Politician: Wealth is relative. If everyone makes a million dollars, you need a million, too—or more. But if everyone makes a tenth of that? You might feel very good about earning that much less.

General: It's the status of the thing.

Politician: Yes, and I know you know about this. Give a military man a specially colored beret, and he is happy and proud. The beret cost ten dollars. But it's worth so much more—beyond all price. That's what I want to bring out. That happiness and pride. It can be done.

Director: You're trying to tame a terrible beast.

Politician: The beast of greed? It can be done—given good laws. The President can't do this. But I, as Speaker, can.

General: There will be a lot of bruised egos.

Politician: And a lot of happy Citizens. I'll take them over the bruised. And who do you think will win?

General: You're very persuasive, which of course is a sort of authority.

Politician: Authority, yes. That's a prize I'll offer to those in healthcare who do well under the new regime.

Director: What about power?

Politician: The power stays with me. I have the power to confer the authority to do certain things. But if the conferees over step their bounds? My power reels them in.

Director: Hmm. I have to admit. I'm having a hard time distinguishing between authority and power.

Politician: Look at it this way. True authority is always legitimate. But power can be problematic.

Director: Why?

Politician: You can have power gotten by illegitimate means.

Director: Would you use such power in the House?

Politician: No, of course not, Director!

General: Liar.

Politician: Ha, ha. True, I'd use every means at my disposal—for the greater good!

Director: General, since he equates the greater good with his good, I think he'd do whatever he could to serve the greater good.

General: That's a very hopeful assessment. What if he's one of the greedy?

Politician: I am. I'm greedy for votes and praise.

Director: I believe that. But limit yourselves to these things—and you'll do well. If you don't...

Politician: What?

Director: ...you're headed for a fall.

Politician: I can live on votes and praise.

Director: But what about your watch? Doesn't that, and things like it, add certain... complications?

Politician: Do you think I don't know? Power, and the authority to use it, are the best accessories, my friend. If the watch, as a metaphor, gets in the way—it's gone.

Director: Which comes first? Power or authority?

Politician: No one will grant you authority if you don't already have power. And if you're given authority first, by some fool chance, there's no guarantee you'll find the power to support it.

Director: And you have power now?

Politician: In the House I do.

Director: And you want the formal authority to rule the House.

Politician: Yes, and you're right—authority is always formal.

General: No, you can have informal authority. You can be listened to, looked to, without a formal role.

Director: He has a point. There's formal authority and informal authority. Power is the thing that seems to me to be neither formal nor informal. Power just is.

Politician: And power always radiates its own natural authority. But there are times when it needs formal authority.

Director: When?

Politician: For example? Why do usurpers always seek a legitimate crown?

Director: Why do they?

Politician: I think it's because they grow tired and think legitimate authority will give them rest.

Director: That could be. And who doesn't need a rest?

20

Politician: Where do you find yours?

Director: In opinion.

Politician: What are you talking about?

Director: Opinion is where philosophers rest.

Politician: Opinion as distinct from knowledge?

Director: Yes, exactly so.

Politician: Why rest in that? Why not rest in the knowledge you have?

Director: Because knowledge is the mine philosophers work.

General: What are you mining for?

Director: Truth. But this metaphor has serious limits. Let's just say philosophers rest in opinion because knowledge is an active thing.

Politician: That makes some sense.

Director: I'm glad you approve.

Politician: Authority that I am?

Director: That was the unspoken thought.

Politician: How short is your rest in opinion?

Director: Just enough to catch my breath.

Politician: And then it's back digging for gold, mining away?

Director: Mining away, yes.

Politician: Like sappers of old?

Director: Are you asking if philosophers undermine things? False authorities, sure. So you'd better be true when it's your time.

Politician: Ha! I'm always true. And I'm sure of the ground on which I stand.

Director: That's good. That's what having authority can do for you. All the power in the world can't make your ground sure.

Politician: That's true. They say power must have eyes on the back of its head. But it can't have eyes beneath its feet!

Director: So is that what authority is? Eyes beneath the feet?

Politician: No. Authority makes those eyes unnecessary. It prevents paranoia. With authority, full authority, you feel—secure.

21

Director: Some say security is an illusion.

Politician: The paranoid think it is.

Director: What's the remedy?

Politician: You might be surprised. You have to allow yourself to be fooled at times—because madness lies the other way.

Director: The paranoid are constantly on guard against being fooled, with everyone and for everything?

Politician: Yes. And with that frame of mind, you're bound to go mad.

General: Director, what does philosophy say about that?

Director: Philosophers are often considered mad—but not because of paranoia.

General: Why are they considered mad?

Director: Because they see illusions almost everywhere they turn.

Politician: And if you turn to me?

Director: You're asking if I see you as an illusion?

Politician: Yes, a fake.

Director: Hmm. Well, it might be an illusion that you're... good.

General: Ha, ha. Yes, I agree. But Director and I are hoping to straighten you out!

Politician: Then I thank you for your efforts.

General: Is he being sarcastic?

Director: No, I think he's serious. Are you, Politician?

Politician: I am. You think I can't take a little constructive criticism? I want to be good, actually good. I want to wear my authority well.

Director: That's a nice turn of phrase. And I believe you mean it. So how to do it?

Politician: Let's ask General. He wears his authority well.

General: Thank you. There's not much to it, really. Just do what you're supposed to do.

Politician: What if people suppose the wrong things?

Director: You'd better educate the People while you still can.

Politician: I have every intention of doing just that. So when the time comes, they'll be ready—for me.

General: What do they need to learn?

Politician: That some politicians are better than others. There's no equality here.

Director: The better are the statesmen?

Politician: Exactly so. And they should be given more leeway, latitude, scope.

Director: What else do the People need to learn?

Politician: That just because something has always been done a certain way, that doesn't mean it's good.

Director: Not good for the times.

Politician: Right.

Director: So you will teach them the times?

Politician: No, they know the times. I will make them aware that there's something to be done.

Director: That something is electing you again and again.

Politician: And I will do what needs to be done.

Director: Why can't others do what needs to be done?

Politician: Oh, there are many reasons. Lack of imagination, cowardice, pig-headed thinking, laziness, vanity—to name a few.

Director: I think that makes sense. And I see none of those things in you. Well, almost none.

Politician: What do you see?

Director: You might be a little... vain.

Politician: Is it vain to know your abilities well, to see them for what they are?

Director: No, I suppose it's not. But you have a lot to live up to in all that you say.

Politician: That spurs me on.

Director: General, what do you think?

General: I think he's speaking truth.

Director: Do you recommend philosophy for him?

General: No.

Politician: I thought everyone could do with a little philosophy.

General: Not everyone, no.

Politician: Why not me?

General: What do you want to learn?

Politician: Learn? Well, nothing.

General: Then there you have it. You know it all.

Politician: Don't mock me.

Director: Maybe we should say you know all you need to know for now.

Politician: That sounds better. How will I know when it's time to learn more?

Director: You'll know. And you'll do it on your own. But if I see you struggling, I'll pay you a visit. But always remember what General said. Do what you're supposed to do. No more, no less.

Politician: I understand 'no less'. But why 'no more'?

Director: One, you don't want to stretch yourself too thin. Two, people don't always appreciate 'more'. Or if they do, it's not in keeping with the effort you put in. But sometimes, hard to believe as it is, they're simply hostile to 'more'.

General: Sometimes you just can't win.

Director: Yes. That's something you need to know, Politician. Not everyone does.

22

Politician: I'll take it under advisement. So, what shall we talk about now? We've got nothing but time.

General: Can we talk about something other than politics?

Politician: Sure! Sports, weather. But what about philosophy? After all, you're a political philosopher, aren't you, Director? That gives us plenty to discuss.

General: What's political philosophy?

Politician: It's philosophy that examines everyday life.

General: Why is that political?

Politician: Because politics is made up of everyday life. How's that for a definition, Director?

Director: Not too bad.

Politician: So let's look at the everyday life of authority. Where does it start?

General: With children looking up to their parents.

Politician: Why do parents have authority over them?

General: Because parents know better than children do.

Politician: Know better to do what?

General: Make decisions.

Politician: So whoever knows how to make good decisions should be given authority?

General: Yes, I think that would serve us all well.

Director: What's a good decision? Sorry if you were already headed there, Politician.

Politician: No, it's fine for you to jump in. General?

General: A good decision is one that benefits those concerned.

Politician: What kind of benefits are we talking about?

General: They could be many.

Politician: Financial?

General: Often times, yes.

Politician: What else?

General: There's safety and security.

Politician: And?

General: You tell us.

Politician: Healthcare for one and all!

Director: Is safety and security more important than healthcare?

Politician: Without it, it's hard to see how we can maintain our health.

Director: And I assume that includes mental health.

Politician: Yes, of course. Chronic lack of safety and security can result in mental illness.

Director: Is this an illness we can cure?

Politician: With time and patience, yes.

Director: And that's the larger goal, to make everyone who is mentally ill well.

Politician: Yes. But let me guess. You're concerned about this goal.

General: Why would anyone be concerned?

Politician: Director is worried mental health will one day lead to thought control.

General: How did you jump to that?

Politician: It's not so big a leap. You know of cognitive behavioral therapy? It suggests that what we think affects our health.

General: That only makes sense.

Politician: Yes. But what if we think thoughts against the government? Might that make us anxious, or depressed?

General: It's hard to know what causes what with these things.

Politician: I agree. But imagine a cognitive behavioral institution run by the government that puts out a schedule of unhealthy thoughts.

General: Yes, I see the problem. People should be free to be unhealthy, if they want.

Politician: But the unhealthy exact a cost on society. They're not as productive. They cause all sorts of minor and not so minor problems. They're a drag.

General: The majority wants to make them healthy like them?

Politician: Yes, assuming the majority is healthy.

General: And if it's not? Would the majority try to make a healthy minority sick like them?

Politician: That's a good question. I don't know. And I hope not to know. I think, for the most part, we're a healthy society.

General: Then it's obvious you don't read the news.

Politician: For every bad story there are a thousand good ones that go untold.

Director: And you will tell their story.

Politician: Yes I will.

Director: You will drape yourself in their flag, so to speak. And you will win, by a thousand to one.

Politician: Well, my opponent will speak to those people, too.

Director: He or she will tell the People's story?

Politician: If they don't tell that story, they'll certainly lose.

Director: But you can rest easy, since you're the best storyteller in the land.

Politician: Now I think you're mocking me.

Director: Political storyteller, I should say.

Politician: I think that's true.

Director: And we all know what people want from their stories.

General: A happy ending.

Director: And the ending here is healthcare for all.

Politician: No one else has been able to do it. I want that to be my legacy. Do you see anything wrong with that?

Director: No, nothing worth arguing here.

Politician: Why would you say that?

Director: You know people will say it's not the government's business to get into all this.

Politician: Of course. That's why I'll offer a hybrid approach. And I'm not going to spell it all out until we're actually working the bills in Congress.

Director: That's only wise. But what will people vote for? A promise?

Politician: They always vote for promises. That's what politics is! And that's why I'm making smaller promises now and fulfilling them all. So when the time comes, people will believe—I can deliver.

23

Director: That sounds okay. I wish you luck.

Politician: Thank you. But what about you? Why don't you get into politics?

Director: Run for office?

Politician: Sure! Why not?

Director: Because that's not where I thrive. You thrive there, so that's where you should be.

General: We should all be where we can thrive.

Director: And that's the secret to knowing how to harmonize people. You put them where they thrive, and that makes for natural harmony with those thriving nearby.

Politician: I didn't know you were such an optimist.

Director: I'm not, really. I'm just describing what you do.

Politician: But if people are thriving isn't that reason to be optimistic?

Director: For every one that thrives, there are probably a dozen who might thrive there, too. Or do you believe we all have our own unique place in the world?

Politician: Well....

Director: Look at you. You might thrive in any number of places. But not everyone can be as flexible as that.

Politician: So what are you suggesting? Some people only have one place where they can thrive? Or are you saying some are so inflexible they can't thrive anywhere they go?

Director: My inclination is to say most people can thrive in several different scenarios. Some people, like you, can thrive in a whole lot more. And others? Maybe they can't thrive at all.

Politician: Yes, I sometimes think that, too. But you're wrong about me.

Director: Oh?

Politician: I'll only truly thrive when I'm Speaker.

Director: No, that's just something you believe. You're thriving now.

Politician: Because I'm on my way.

Director: Maybe so. But don't be so wedded to the idea of your end that you miss out on other good things in life.

Politician: I make it a point not to miss out. Not missing out puts me in the frame of mind to win.

General: Are you really that single-minded?

Politician: I'm focused, General. Focused

General: What happens if you never make it to Speaker?

Politician: After trying and trying again? I supposed I'd have to settle for President.

General: Ha! And I think you're serious!

Director: He certainly has the self-belief it takes.

Politician: It's not so much self-belief as it is self-authority.

Director: Self-authority?

Politician: Some people brag they have self-control. But that can't give them a clear conscience as they tell themselves what to do. That's what self-authority does.

Director: It blesses your deeds.

Politician: Yes. You have a clear conscience as you tell yourself what to do.

Director: And you know all your commands are legit.

Politician: Exactly.

General: Legit with you. But what about with the electorate?

Politician: They sometimes take persuading. And what's more persuasive than having authority over yourself?

Director: I like this self-authority. But I'd use it for something else.

Politician: What, Director?

Director: Thought. I'd authorize each and every thought I might have.

Politician: You'd consider each thought true?

Director: You show how little you know about thinking, if you'll excuse me for saying.

Politician: Of course I will! I want to learn. So tell us more.

Director: It's not about truth. It's about freedom. We make much of freedom of speech. And this, of course, is good. But before there can be freedom of speech there must be freedom of thought.

Politician: That only makes sense. But who is stopping us from thinking?

Director: Authorities.

Politician: Which authorities?

Director: Any of them.

Politician: You can't paint with so broad a brush.

Director: Why not? Tell me of an authority that doesn't interfere with thought.

Politician: I'm an authority in my role in the House. I'm not stopping anyone from thinking.

Director: Of course you are. You make things look so easy, when I know full well how hard you try. So certain people look at you and think, 'Hey, that doesn't seem so hard. I could do that.' They never think about what it takes.

Politician: Oh, that's nonsense. If that's all I do, then I'd say I'm not so bad.

Director: Yes, but as an authority people look to you, when maybe they should be looking someplace else.

Politician: To philosophy?

Director: Yes.

Politician: But I could say the same of you. People look to philosophy when maybe they should be looking at me!

Director: Yes, but philosophy isn't an authority.

Politician: What is it?

Director: A certain kind of life.

Politician: You can't tell me all those weighty tomes aren't authorities.

Director: They become authorities when philosophy dies. I would keep it alive.

Politician: How can I help you do this?

Director: Resign and live this life.

Politician: Ha! And you were telling me how good I am.

Director: You are. But there are better things in life.

Politician: Like sitting around and talking all night?

Director: That's something I enjoy. You appear to be enjoying it, too.

Politician: That's because we're stuck in this storm, and I'm too tired from the day to do any work. This talk is charging me back up. Nothing more, nothing less.

Director: Well, you asked how you can help. If you find someone else who charges you up, put them in touch with me.

Politician: Why? You're going to recruit them?

Director: I think it takes a special sort of person to charge you up. Oh, I know you get charged from the crowds. But I'm looking for individuals. Send them to me and I will learn what makes them tick. And this can make me helpful to you.

Politician: How?

Director: I might find 'chargers' to send to you, based on what I learn.

Politician: You're like any philosopher. You want to get people who are affiliated with you into positions of power. You want to change the world.

Director: Don't you?

Politician: Yes! But on my own terms!

Director: The chargers will be operating strictly on your terms.

Politician: Then what's in it for you?

Director: Like I said, I'll get to learn. And who knows? One day I might need a favor. Nothing says philosophers can't be prudent—so long as prudence doesn't trump philosophy.

24

General: Give us an example of when philosophy trumps prudence.

Director: I'm in a meeting with my boss and my peers. My boss makes an observation about human nature that doesn't ring true. Prudence might dictate I bite my tongue. Don't make waves, as they say. But philosophy begs me to differ.

Politician: Do you differ?

Director: I do.

Politician: Do you differ often?

Director: Oh, who can say how often 'often' is?

Politician: I'll take that as a yes. Why haven't you been fired for all the differing you do?

Director: Because I'm prudent.

Politician: How so?

Director: I do all the things my boss can't do, and give him the credit. But tell us, Politician. When do you differ?

Politician: Haven't you heard me speak? I differ with the opposing party. I differ with my party!

Director: Yes, but when do you differ with the electorate? Or are you simply their tool, a puppet of their will?

Politician: You can't provoke me, Director. So don't even try.

Director: But I have to try—in order to prove your mettle. So what do you say, Politician? How do you differ? Perhaps they think their interests are one thing but you know they're another, and so you argue with them?

Politician: They know their interests full well.

Director: So there's no arguing here. But perhaps you differ with them on how you should champion these interests?

Politician: There's truth in that. I often know best and have to argue the point.

Director: So that's how you differ. You argue with them on how to give them what they want.

Politician: Look. You're making me out like I'm some slave. That's hardly the case. I get what I want, too. Slaves don't get what they want. I do.

Director: Okay. Everyone gets what they want. Except... for the minority. What do you do about the minority? Shuffle them aside?

Politician: I find ways to serve their interests, too.

Director: What if it's a minority of one? Do you even care?

Politician: Of course I care.

Director: What will you do?

Politician: Serve them, too.

Director: That's an awful lot of constituent service from a man who needs to focus on national healthcare reform.

Politician: That's why I have a staff.

Director: That helps you on healthcare reform.

Politician: What's your point? Life isn't perfect, Director.

Director: Yes, but when I was in the army we talked about leaving no one behind.

Politician: Then I will leave no one behind.

Director: That's a very big promise from an ambitious man.

Politician: What does ambition have to do with this?

Director: The ones behind might slow you down.

Politician: Nonsense.

Director: Do you think they'll speed you up?

Politician: If I show care to those left behind, the others will know I'm for real.

Director: So it's prudent to show care.

Politician: He's a clever devil, isn't he, General?

General: He's clever, but he's only speaking truth.

Politician: Is it prudent for you to show care?

General: It's my duty. Prudent or not.

Director: Yes, but politicians need to be prudent. There must be no shame in this. General, do you agree?

General: I know enough about politics to say that's so.

Director: Such a nice dovetailing of traits.

Politician: What are you talking about?

Director: Your desire to win, your desire to do well for those you serve, your desire for everyone to love you for being such a good guy.

Politician: I know you're teasing, testing me. But I admit all of that is true.

Director: If you had to pick one, which would it be?

Politician: My desire to do well for those I serve.

Director: Even if it means you lose?

Politician: Yes.

Director: Even if you're not loved?

Politician: Yes.

General: But if he does well for those he serves, he knows full well it will lead him to win. And if he wins and thrives? He'll be loved.

25

Politician: So you see I chose well.

Director: I'd say you're an authority on such choices.

General: And I'd say you, Director, are an authority on choices, too.

Director: Oh? What choices?

General: What words to speak.

Director: What makes you think that?

General: Your words are to the point.

Director: If they are it's because I know I'll never have this chance again.

Politician: What chance?

Director: The two of you here tonight in this storm.

Politician: What do you hope to do with this chance?

Director: Learn all I can. You two couldn't possibly occupy the positions you do without knowing much. Could you?

Politician: I think you're mocking again. What do philosophers say? All I know is that I know nothing?

Director: I don't say that. I know a thing or two.

Politician: What thing or two do you know?

Director: I know that you need to get rid of your final self-doubt.

Politician: And what doubt is that?

Director: That it will all be for nothing.

Politician: Ha! It's already not for nothing. But what about General? Does he have a final self-doubt?

Director: Of course. That he could have done more.

General: It's true. But I can never be rid of this doubt.

Politician: Why not?

General: It's because... because....

Director: Because it's who he is.

General: Yes.

Politician: Why doesn't he doubt that it's all been for nothing?

General: You can only ask that question because you weren't there.

Politician: You fulfilled your responsibilities, so it can't be for nothing. I get that. But what responsibilities do I have?

General: I'm not sure you get it. But I'll answer your question. You have responsibility for your promises. You can't make them lightly.

Politician: Can I make them lightly if I take them seriously afterwards?

General: Why would you do that?

Politician: Because I don't want to seem too serious, too heavy. It's part of my image to appear effortless. People like that.

General: People like when you work hard for them.

Politician: Not really. People like success. If it seems to come easily, so much the better.

Director: Why is it better?

Politician: Because then they think you can easily do more.

General: But you can't.

Politician: You underestimate my capacity for work.

General: Maybe. But there's a limit. What then?

Politician: I enlist others to the cause.

General: And if it's all too much for them?

Director: Politician will need to gauge how much they can take before he opens his mouth.

Politician: Open my mouth?

Director: With promises.

Politician: Believe me, I gauge quite a bit before I 'open my mouth'. Always. You should do the same.

Director: I agree. But let's be clear. Do you gauge how much truth people can take?

Politician: I do.

Director: Why?

Politician: Because people can't always handle the truth. But that's your job, too. You're an authority here as a philosopher, right?

Director: An authority on truth? No, Politician. I'm a seeker after truth.

General: Yes, Director. But philosophers deal expertly in truth. Doesn't that make them among the greatest of authorities here?

Director: There have been philosophers who have had great authority, and there have been philosophers who have had no authority.

General: What makes the difference?

Director: I think it's mostly luck, in the sense of circumstance.

Politician: What kind of luck do you have?

Director: As you see.

General: Ha, ha. Good answer.

Politician: Why do I get the sense the military man and the thinker are teamed up against the statesman?

Director: Congratulations on the promotion.

General: Congratulations, Statesman!

Politician: Do you seriously doubt I'm a statesman and not a mere politician?

Director: That remains to be seen. If you can pass your healthcare legislation you might very well be a statesman.

Politician: Not 'might very well be'—'certainly be'.

Director: Alright, you'd certainly be a statesman. But is that what a statesman is? Someone who knows how to count votes?

Politician: You think passing legislation is easy?

Director: I don't know. You and your kind want to make it look easy. So I must ask myself, 'How hard can it be?'

Politician: Try trading hundreds of favors and see how easy it is.

Director: So you're an authority on trading favors? Is that what it's all about?

Politician: That's why they call it politics.

General: That makes no sense. Really, Politician. What are you an authority on?

Politician: Getting things done. And you? What are you an authority on?

General: Getting things done, in order to win.

Politician: Well, that's exactly what I do. But Director never gets to win. When is the last time you heard of a philosopher winning?

Director: Winning isn't the point.

Politician: What is the point? Oh, wait. I forgot. There is no point! Ha, ha!

General: Director, seriously. What's the point of philosophy?

Director: To guide me on my way.

Politician: And all of philosophy serves you?

Director: Yes. But before you tell me I'm arrogant, let me say a few words. All of philosophy must be reborn in each philosopher or else it dies—though there is a chance it will be found by accident some day and be brought back to life.

Politician: And so what if philosophy dies? I'll still pass my healthcare legislation and all will be well.

General: I'm a firm believer in diversity. And if philosophers die out, there goes another species. Am I right?

Director: You're right.

Politician: If philosophers go the way of the dinosaurs, I'm fine with that—since that's what they are.

Director: You say with that such authority. General, do you know the only way he could say that with more authority?

General: No, how?

Director: If he were handsome.

Politician: What! Ha, ha! What are you talking about?

Director: Don't you know the one thing you're missing that would make your authority complete? Good looks.

Politician: You should talk. You're the most average looking man I think I've ever seen. Then again, maybe you fall a touch on the ugly side, like me.

Director: Yes, but a little 'ugly' with the right kind of power goes a long way. But seriously, good looks confer a certain kind of authority, don't they?

Politician: Not at all. Lookers don't have to try as hard. Everyone knows it. So, if anything, it's harder to achieve authority when you have good looks— because people assume you don't deserve what you've got.

Director: I don't know, Politician. I've seen people hang on every word one of the beautiful people speaks. If that's not authority, I don't know what is.

General: But what is beauty? They say it's in the eye of the beholder.

Politician: Behold my natural authority and see the beauty.

Director: Wait a minute. I need to find my glasses.

Politician: Oh, come on! Some people are meant to command.

General: There's truth to that. But command proper takes a whole lot of training.

Politician: That's what my career has been up until now. What training do you have, Director?

Director: People try to school me nearly every day. But I'm afraid I never learn.

General: What do they try to school you in?

Director: How to be more of an authority.

Politician: Oh, no one's schooling you on that. But don't you have the authority of reason? Aren't you all set?

Director: I'll forget you're forgetting what we said about this. The authority of reason is a funny thing.

Politician: Funny? Why?

Director: Because some people pay no heed to reason at all, while others worship it blindly.

Politician: I know the first type all too well. But say more about the second. What's wrong with worshipping reason? Isn't that what you want? Blindly or not?

Director: Anyone who worships reason doesn't know what reason is.

Politician: What is reason? Isn't it truly the ultimate authority? Even I'm subject to reason.

General: There's reason to all of my commands.

Director: Would you say you worship reason, General?

General: Maybe not worship. Respect. I respect reason and expect reason of myself.

Politician: We're in complete agreement here.

Director: Why do you respect reason, General?

General: It has to do with justice.

Director: Can you say more?

General: Reason, when it's not mere argument, does justice to whatever it touches.

Politician: Touches. I like that.

Director: What is justice?

General: Love of truth.

Director: So to do justice to something is to tell the truth about it.

General: Yes.

Director: If you have a good soldier beneath you, you do justice through praise?

General: Yes.

Director: And if you have a bad soldier, you do justice through blame?

General: I do. I tell it like it is. That's something Politician can rarely do.

Politician: Oh, you'd be surprised what truth I speak behind closed doors.

Director: You don't speak truth to the electorate?

Politician: Of course I do. I tell them only truth—just not all of it.

Director: Some people would call that a lie.

Politician: People who don't know what reason is, yes.

Director: You can reason without complete information?

Politician: Ha! As if you don't know what that's all about.

General: If I reason without complete information, people die.

Politician: No one's talking about giving you incomplete relevant information, General.

Director: 'Relevant' being the operative word?

Politician: That's what politics is, Director. The art of the relevant.

Director: I thought it was the art of the possible.

Politician: Nothing is possible if you don't know what's relevant to whom.

Director: Is that a sort of doing justice to them?

Politician: Hmm. That's an interesting question. I think the answer is yes.

General: Don't do that kind of justice to me. I want full information.

Politician: Is it relevant to you to know that I had to twist a Representative's arm to get her to vote in favor of funding for you?

General: Well....

Politician: Yes, 'well'. It might make things harder on you in dealing with her—to no good purpose.

Director: That was well said and with authority, Politician.

Politician: Only because I'm speaking truth. But there are things you and I would speak of, General, that I wouldn't tell her. It goes both ways.

Director: Except you're in on it every way.

Politician: That's why I deserve to speak for the House. I know what needs to be said and done.

Director: That may be the definition.

Politician: What definition?

Director: Of authority. Authority is knowing what needs to be said and done. What do you think?

General: Yes, Director, that makes good sense. But there's a difficulty. There are plenty of people in positions of authority who don't know what needs to be said and done.

Politician: They have false authority. Or maybe I should say they don't wear authority well. They don't belong where they are. They should be removed.

Director: Will you remove them when you Speak?

Politician: To the extent it's humanly possible, I swear I will.

Director: You've just won my vote.

General: And mine.

Politician: Well, it only took half an evening to do it! Ha, ha! Thanks, my friends.

Director: Are you friends with all who vote for you?

Politician: Are you trying to make me blush? There are friends, and then there are friends. You two are the latter.

Director: I'm not sure what that means, but thanks nonetheless. This feeling of gratitude you create must serve you well.

Politician: It does.

Director: What's the secret? How do you do it?

Politician: Oh, it's an old trick. You make the person you're talking to feel like they're the only person in the world. If there are two people, those two are the only two people in the world. If there are a hundred, the same. And so on, and so on.

General: What if you're addressing the world?

Politician: I'm speaking to each and every one as if they're the only one. You have to reach the heart.

Director: And you can do this because your heart is the same as theirs?

Politician: No, I wouldn't say that. It's because I have insight into the human psyche.

Director: I wish I had that insight.

General: Philosophers don't?

Director: Philosophers more often than not get caught struggling on the surface, far away from insight.

Politician: Why do you think that is?

Director: Because philosophers are often literalists.

General: What does that mean?

Director: The literal is the surface meaning of words. Philosophers, being very polite, refuse to assume they know what lies beneath. So they have to ask. If someone shares what's in their depths, the philosopher will be duly impressed. Not everyone is willing to share, after all.

Politician: And when they ask the philosopher what's in his depths?

Director: 'His' being me?

Politician: Yes. What's in your depths, Director?

Director: I don't know. I can't see that well down there. But maybe with your insight into the human psyche you can tell me.

Politician: An artful dodge. But I think I know your secret. Are you ready?

Director: Ready if not willing.

Politician: Your secret is—frustrated ambition.

Director: And is that the secret of all philosophers?

Politician: I think it is.

Director: So if you fail to become Speaker, you'll turn to philosophy for consolation?

Politician: I won't fail.

Director: Okay. It would probably be too late for you, anyway.

General: Why would it be too late? Can't we all seek consolation no matter our age?

Director: Yes we can. But let me be serious for a moment. Philosophy isn't about consolation for frustrated ambition, or frustrated anything else for that matter.

Politician: Then what's it about?

Director: Trying to find a way.

Politician: Not The Way?

Director: No, not that way. A way.

Politician: A way to what?

General: I know what. A way to hope.

Politician: Hope? I deal in hope. What does Director know about hope?

Director: I know it when I find it.

General: And that's the most important search there is. We're nothing without hope.

Politician: While that's true, I think Director is leading us astray.

Director: How?

Politician: Philosophy has to be more than the search for hope. For instance, what does it do when it finds it?

Director: I should have been more clear. I'm hopeful I'll find hope.

Politician: Now you're being ridiculous.

General: No. I think I understand. He's talking about the difference between external and internal hope. Am I right?

Director: I'm not sure. I never thought about it that way before. Can you say more?

General: Internally, you hope you'll find hope in others, the external hope.

Director: There's sense in what you say.

Politician: What are the grounds for the internal hope?

Director: One foot is planted on experience; the other on reason.

Politician: But what does that have to do with hope?

Director: Experience shows hope is possible.

Politician: But what if in your experience you never had hope?

Director: You've almost certainly seen it in others.

Politician: Then what does reason do?

Director: It plots a likely course to find it.

Politician: That's it? Plots a likely course?

Director: It's better than the alternative.

General: No, Director is right. So many do nothing. He is talking about doing something.

Politician: Now I see why you two aren't in politics. I have to do more than 'something'. I have to deliver.

Director: But now I'm confused. Hopes are what you deal in, no?

Politician: Of course. But I only raise them when I know what needs to be done to meet them.

Director: You don't always know?

Politician: You of all people should know that knowing is hard.

General: But what's harder still is knowing but not being able to do anything about it.

Director: So the trick is to know, raise hopes, then do something about it. Or should you only raise hopes once you're done?

Politician: That's a luxury no politician can afford.

Director: So you have to gamble, bet that you can do it.

Politician: Precisely. Is that how it is with philosophy?

Director: Does philosophy make bets? I suppose it does, in a small way. But not really large bets, no. At least not me.

Politician: No? Isn't the bet that you're not wasting your life on nonsense a large one?

Director: Well, when you put it like that you force me to own I might reconsider.

Politician: 'Force me to own I might reconsider.' What a phrase! So you're thinking maybe you're making a large bet with your life?

Director: I've thought about it, and no—no large bet. Many small bets. A great many small bets. More than most make, I'd venture.

General: What kind of small bets, Director?

Director: Gambles on choosing just the right words for the situation.

Politician: Because if you choose the wrong word catastrophe follows? I deal in words. And while I certainly don't want to put my foot in my mouth—

Director: What does that phrase mean?

Politician: Excuse me?

Director: Foot in the mouth. Where does that come from? Why the foot? Why not put your thumb in your mouth?

General: Ha, ha! Yes, why not?

Politician: Ha, ha. But as I was saying, there's a certain flexibility in these things. There are red lines you can't cross, certainly. But words aren't as important as some people think.

Director: I think they're very important. In fact, I'd say words are the ultimate authority.

Politician: Now why would you say that?

Director: Because words are how we think.

General: But then words are just tools. The thinking is the authority.

Director: But when we've thought we deliver what we think in words.

Politician: True. But do we only deliver to others, or do we deliver to ourselves?

Director: Both.

General: Words can be a sort of invasion.

Politician: What are you talking about?

General: They invade our mind and we're forced to deal with them. If we don't, bad things happen.

Director: I agree. Some words invade; others we let in through the front door— gladly.

General: Yes, that's a good point. But we still have to deal with them.

Director: And we deal with them as friends.

Politician: Well, I'm glad to see such harmony here. But I want to get back to the thoughts we deliver in words. If they are backed by reason, by good thinking, they have authority.

Director: To some. To others they mean nothing.

General: There's nothing more true. And it gets back to justice again. Those who care about justice will feel the authority of reasoned words; those who don't, won't.

Politician: You think it's that simple?

General: It is.

Politician: But people have crazy notions of justice. People think justice is getting what you deserve. And you know what some people think they deserve! What do you make of this, Director?

Director: I'm inclined to side with General here. Words, authority, and justice are of a piece.

Politician: And what about what people deserve?

Director: Some would say there's an Authority that gives us all what we deserve. But I don't believe in that.

26

Politician: 'God' is the highest Authority there ever was.

Director: Just to be sure—do you believe?

Politician: I don't believe.

Director: But many people want you to believe, don't they?

Politician: They do. I simply tell them I was raised in the faith but no longer practice.

Director: So you lie to them. You let them believe you believe.

Politician: If letting believe is to lie then we're all big liars here.

Director: I try to be as little a liar as I can. And I want people to know, not believe.

Politician: Yes, yes, I know—that's what philosophy is.

General: Getting people to know?

Politician: Right.

General: Director, is that what philosophy is?

Director: I'm inclined to agree—but with a reservation.

Politician: What reservation?

Director: We have to know what knowledge is. And that, my friend, requires considerable discussion.

General: I don't see why.

Politician: Oh, he means something like this. We once 'knew' the Earth was flat. And some day we might come to 'know' the Earth isn't actually round. Certain physicists already suspect this truth. The point is that knowledge is problematic. But so what? We know what we know when we know it. That's it.

General: So knowledge is something that works for a time?

Politician: The whole universe is only for a time.

Director: Then I don't understand how you can project a goal so far into the future not knowing what might change.

Politician: What, the Speakership? Things change, but only over time. If anything starts to change, I'll adjust.

Director: I do marvel at your confidence.

Politician: I simply keep a watchful eye on the horizon.

General: As must I.

Director: I'm too busy toiling away at my work.

Politician: Yes, but I know you. You see the horizon through the eyes of your friends.

Director: That's true. But when I see something concerning, I look up and see for myself. Then I tell my friend the horizon might not show what they think. And we investigate together.

Politician: Why not always look up and see for yourself.

Director: I don't know what the signs on the horizon mean.

Politician: I doubt that. I think you're rather astute.

Director: I honestly don't know what they mean. But if you and I are talking, and you say X is on the horizon and this means Y for you, I'll have a look. And if it doesn't look like an X to me but rather an A, I'll tell you and try to show you what I mean.

Politician: And then you'll tell me what it means for me?

Director: No, because I really don't know. But I'll explain to you that it's not X-means-Y. It could mean A-means-Y, who knows? That's for you to decide. I just point out what I can see.

Politician: Why can't you see the connection between the two?

Director: Because I'm so focused on A-means-A that I can't.

General: I don't understand.

Director: Some people will try to tell you that A means B, or C, and so on. But a philosopher knows the only thing A means is A.

Politician: That sounds like a liability for philosophy.

Director: Not to friends I've helped by thinking this way.

Politician: But what are you saying? Is it this? I might say, A, it's clear the electorate always believes in men like me; which means, B, I will be Speaker. And you might say, 'That's not clear.'

Director: Yes, that sounds like something I might say.

Politician: Well, I'm saying it now. What do you say?

Director: Let me look up and see the horizon. Hmm. I see excited voters, hyped up on promises. I see you looking confident and strong. I see votes coming your way. Your position in Congress seems strong. But I see jealous Party members working the backchannels to undermine your elevation to Speaker, to undermine your authority. That's as far as I can see. So it doesn't seem like A-means-B to me, not necessarily.

General: That's because Politician must serve two masters. People and Party.

Politician: But the Party serves the People, so it works out well.

Director: Hmm. I'm looking up at the horizon....

Politician: Oh, stop it. I know there are tensions here. Sometimes the Party serves the Party.

General: The Party always serves the Party. That's what parties are for!

Director: Yes, General. That's a very good point. So Politician must rise above party.

Politician: And I do.

General: But still, they have their tentacles on you.

Politician: Like you said, I serve two masters.

General: No one can serve two masters and thrive.

Politician: It happens every day.

Director: So your task isn't that difficult?

Politician: Ha, ha. With enough authority? It's not.

General: But gaining that authority, that dual authority, is very difficult.

Politician: Nothing more difficult, yes.

Director: General, do you need dual authority?

General: Of course I do. Up and down the chain of command.

Director: The down chain is military; and the up chain is political?

General: Yes.

Director: I'd say you have it harder than Politician. Both of his positions of authority are political. One type of thing is generally easier to deal with than two.

Politician: Yes, but the 'down' for General is by and large monolithic. My 'down', the People, is a hyper-variegated mess!

Director: Are citizens really all that different when it comes down to it? I thought they all want the same thing.

General: Yes, and it's a mistake to think all soldiers are alike. We have more variety than you think.

Politician: Okay, okay. I stand corrected. But it's the same with the Party. They don't all think the same thing. I have to suss each one of them out and see what needs to be done.

Director: Do you treat the important Party members as individuals and the hyper-variegated people as so many groups?

Politician: I have to. There simply isn't time.

Director: So what kind of authority does that make you?

Politician: What do you mean?

Director: Up the chain you're an authority with individuals. Down the chain you're an authority with electoral groups.

Politician: If you know of a better way, I'm all ears.

Director: I don't know of a better way. I think it's a limit of our system, our way of life.

General: Are you suggesting the system forces us into a certain way of life?

Director: Are you suggesting it doesn't?

Politician: What are the consequences of this way of life?

Director: On the whole, they're not too bad. More is done for the Party than the People, yes. But the People get a touch of justice, too.

General: They need much more than a touch.

Director: That would mean Politician would have to spend more time with the People than the Party.

Politician: But keeping the Party at bay helps me serve the People. And do you know what happens if once I'm in and I only focus on the People?

Director: Justice?

Politician: No! Tyranny.

General: Oh, come on. Serving the People isn't tyranny.

Politician: I can see you don't know your history very well. Tyrants start out as champions of the people. Then they overthrow the powers that be. Then they're in total control.

Director: Who is your non-tyrannical legislative model?

Politician: Henry Clay. He worked it both up and down and stayed within the system.

Director: That's a fine model to pick. Though he lost the Presidential race several times.

Politician: He should have stayed content within the House.

Director: Remind me. Why Speaker and not President?

Politician: Laws. We are a nation of laws. The President passes no laws. Yes, he or she signs or vetoes. But Congress can override the latter. Presidents merely enforce laws, or should.

Director: You don't have to go to law school to know what you're saying is true. But why are so many fixated on the Presidency?

Politician: They see it as the highest authority in the land.

General: I thought the Supreme Court was the highest authority in the land.

Politician: In many ways, it is. But the President garners the most attention. He acts alone. The Court acts with many Justices, and Congress with a great many more Congresspeople.

Director: That's the allure, to act alone?

Politician: The allure and the illusion, too. No President can act alone.

General: But the ultimate decision is theirs.

Politician: True, but if you've seen these people up close and personal, you know they don't want to act wholly alone.

General: But they have the authority to do so.

Politician: Not all of us want to live up to our authority.

Director: Why not?

Politician: Haven't you ever heard it's lonely at the top?

General: Yes, of course. But sometimes you do have to act alone. I do, often—after I receive advice.

Politician: Well, Presidents want more than advice. They want people to blame, people to take the fall—if it comes to that. And it often does.

Director: So you don't want to play that game of blame and fall?

Politician: The voters play it for me. I speak to them and let them decide.

Director: Decide on the worth of your peers.

Politician: Why else command the national stage? It gives me authority over my peers. They know I can help or harm, as I see fit.

General: And that gives you leverage to pass healthcare reform.

Politician: Yes, but I'll be honest. It's much more than healthcare reform. It's healthcare creation. We don't have a system now. We have some kind of ugly de facto conglomeration. Do you know how many arms I'll have to twist?

Director: Let me see if I understand. It's your authority that will let you twist their arms?

Politician: No, I'll twist them through brute force. My authority is what will prevent them from complaining.

Director: Interesting. How does that work?

Politician: When you have real authority, the People can't believe you're capable of that, the brute force. So no one complains.

Director: What would happen if they did, anyway?

Politician: No one would believe them. They'd think they're being cry babies, for lack of a better word.

Director: Because they didn't get their way.

Politician: Yes. And there's more to it than that. The arm twisting usually involves ugly things, things no one wants to let see the light of day. That keeps them quiet, too.

General: Cry babies with guilty consciences. Ha! I'm glad you can keep them in line. But that must mean you have a clean conscience. Otherwise, they'd prey on you.

Politician: Exactly. That's how I can have the confidence I do.

Director: Is there a difference between having a clean conscience and never having done something that's usually perceived as wrong?

Politician: What kind of question is that?

General: Have you done things that are usually perceived as wrong?

Politician: Haven't we all? But perceived-as-wrong is different than wrong.

General: Not in politics.

Politician: You have a point, of course. That's why they say perception is reality.

Director: But we three know reality is reality.

General: A is A.

Director: Nicely put. But as you climb the political heights I think it's easy to lose sight of that basic fact.

Politician: I'm in the heights and I haven't lost sight.

Director: But you're not in the highest height. Power or authority, and the highest power or authority, don't differ in degree; they differ in quality; they differ in type.

Politician: And you're saying I'll change when I reach that highest height.

Director: It's certainly happened before.

Politician: So what should I do? I have to play the cards I've been dealt. And if I say so myself, I have a very good hand.

27

Director: Poker, yes. That's the national game. It involves bluffing and playing on other's confidence and greed. You draw them in slowly when you have a very good hand. Sweetening the pot, as they say. But there comes a time when you need to know to fold.

Politician: Are you seriously implying I should get out of politics?

Director: No. But you have to keep your mind open to the possibility that one day that day will come.

Politician: My mind is always open. But I don't think that day is coming any time soon.

Director: You know better than I. So sweeten the pot. And come what may.

General: I sometimes play poker with the enemy.

Director: You mean you bluff?

General: Of course I bluff. I also try to draw them in.

Politician: Do philosophers bluff?

Director: I suppose some do, for the sake of the cause.

General: Do you?

Director: Not as a rule.

Politician: Not as a rule? Ha! You always lose if you bluff as a rule. But do you bluff on occasion?

Director: I'd rather not. Would you?

Politician: Rather not bluff? Of course. But sometimes when your hand is weak you must. If you want to stay in the game.

Director: That's the thing. I'm not trying to stay in any game. If the game comes to me, that's great, or at least pretty good, I think. But if it doesn't? I don't go chasing it around, puffing myself up.

Politician: I'm not chasing the game. The game came to me.

Director: I somehow doubt it's as clear as all that.

General: Yes, Politician. Certainly you at least met it halfway.

Politician: Fair enough. But I will never chase. I might woo, and maybe bluff a little now and then. But chase? No.

Director: You'll force the game to come to you. After all, what's the arm twisting for?

Politician: Arm twisting is necessary for people who don't know how the game is played.

Director: They think their weak hands should win?

Politician: Exactly. I show them the rules.

Director: And the rules are the authority in the game.

Politician: That's right.

Director: Who makes the rules?

Politician: No one. The rules just are.

Director: Haven't you heard of statesmen who changed the rules?

Politician: Well, yes. But you can only do that when you have a solid command of the rules as they exist.

Director: Having this solid command will give you authority?

Politician: Yes.

Director: What if you try to change the rules without having this authority?

Politician: You mean you try to change them through brute force?

Director: Yes, what then?

Politician: You might succeed. But then you've set up a dictatorship of sorts.

Director: The dictator has no real authority?

Politician: Not legitimate authority.

Director: General, would you follow the orders of a dictator?

General: Of course not.

Director: Why not?

General: Because the dictator lacks proper authority. Without that, I don't listen.

Director: I'd hate to see what happens when you don't listen.

General: So would I.

Director: Politician, what would you do if faced with such a dictator?

Politician: I'd seek to remove him or her from power.

Director: Through any legitimate means?

Politician: Through any means to restore the proper order.

Director: I suppose you'd find an ally in General?

General: I would seek legitimate means. If we make use of illegitimate means, what's left when we've won?

Director: Yes, a good question. And we're sure dictators have no authority?

Politician: No legitimate authority.

Director: So they do have authority?

Politician: Of course they do.

Director: When challenging the authority of a dictator, we could use help, couldn't we?

Politician: Certainly. What kind of people do you have in mind?

Director: Those with experience challenging dictators.

Politician: What, some kind of a foreigners from a tyrannical land?

Director: Sure, but I was thinking about something closer to home. Where do you think we form our earliest dispositions toward authority?

General: As we said. At home. Our parents are our earliest authorities.

Politician: And sometimes there's a parent who is a positive dictator. Is that your point, Director?

Director: That's a point, for sure. What's success when challenging dictatorial authority?

Politician: Living to tell about it.

General: Often times children run away.

Director: What stops them?

General: Fear. Love. Hope.

Director: You can love a dictator, can't you?

General: Yes, you can.

Director: Do you think a true dictator, in the political sense, can sense this about someone—that they've loved a minor dictator?

General: I bet they can tell. And they'd like that about them.

Director: So we should look for someone who once loved a dictator, but knows the political dictator has to go. That's our way in.

Politician: And if they come to love dictatorship again?

Director: Well, you raise an interesting question. What do they love? The dictator, or the dictatorship?

Politician: I would argue you can't separate the two. It's the combination that creates the authority.

General: But there's a problem. Won't this person of ours fear authority? You can love and fear at once, you know.

Politician: Yes, and you can love, fear, and respect at once, as well. That combination would be very appealing to a dictator in full power. So why would this person of ours do it? Why fight the dictator's authority?

Director: Because they grew up and learned the truth. Dictatorship isn't good.

Politician: But it isn't always... bad.

General: What do you mean?

Politician: Sometimes in times of crisis a dictator must arise, to take control and restore some semblance of order.

General: I don't buy it. That's the oldest political argument there is.

Politician: But it's true. We've just been fortunate enough never to have needed one, though at times we came quite close.

General: Director?

Director: Who can say what's needed in times of civil unrest or awful war? I would prefer not to live under a dictator because his or her very existence means things have gone terribly wrong.

Politician: Well, who can argue with that? But it is interesting to see how children's relationships with parental authority shape their outlook to authority in general. Good parental authority makes for a trusting attitude toward other authority.

General: Oh, that's not always true. We can just as easily say good parental authority makes you highly suspicious of any authority that seems less than good. It's the same with bad parental authority. That might predispose you to hate all authority, or it might leave you hungering for an authority of even the slightest goodness.

Politician: Well, you make a good point. Who knows what we learn as kids? There are a lot of variables in play.

Director: Does authority ever play?

General: Play as in have fun? I'm not so sure it does—at least not well.

Politician: I'm an authority and I can be playful.

General: Not while you're actually engaged in being an authority.

Politician: Of course I can!

General: Give an example.

Politician: While chairing a committee hearing I can have some fun, be a little playful—as I was this morning with you! Have you forgotten already?

General: Of course not. But at that moment you were no longer an authority. You stepped out of role. Then you stepped right back in.

Director: Can dictators step out of their role?

Politician: No doubt. And when they can it's very sweet for them. It takes having the right audience.

Director: An outsider, no?

Politician: Yes, that's what it usually is.

General: Was I an outsider to you today?

Politician: Was I a dictator to you?

General: You supply the means that keep my troops alive. That's some serious authority. But are you a dictator? No.

Politician: You were an outsider in the sense that you don't belong to the capital. So I had a little fun with you.

Director: But would it have come off as well if General had tried to have a little fun with you?

Politician: It depends on the fun.

Director: Yes, I think it does. What kind of fun is allowed?

Politician: Fun that respects the authority of the committee. If anyone is going to mock that authority, it's got to be me.

Director: Does that respect have to extend to the chair of the committee?

Politician: Are you asking if I'm always to be respected? When I'm acting in my formal capacity? Yes. Outside of that? No, of course not.

Director: Are dictators always respected, formally or not?

Politician: They almost always demand to be respected by all in every situation.

Director: Why?

Politician: Because they're vulnerable.

Director: And you're not?

Politician: If I am what happens to me? I might lose a vote in the House. A dictator gets hung by his neck to die through his vulnerabilities.

Director: You might lose a vote because of disrespect?

Politician: The more power you have the more respect you can command. If you don't have the power you might still command the respect. That gives you the appearance of power.

Director: I'm following you. But why lose the vote?

Politician: Disrespect suggests you're lacking in power. That suggestion inclines politicians to vote as they please and not as you want.

Director: I see. But if you have the power, regardless of disrespect, you can make them vote as you want. No?

Politician: Yes, but power is a funny thing. Sometimes the appearance of power is power. And you can lose the power you have if people don't believe you have it.

Director: Tell us something. Is authority power?

Politician: Authority is a sign of power.

Director: Thanks. I just wanted that to be clear.

General: Why?

Director: Because when ambitious people seek, sometimes they seek power, and sometimes they seek authority. What kind of person seeks authority over power?

Politician: A fool.

Director: And what kind of person seeks power over authority?

Politician: A happy one. But now you tell us why this is.

Director: Because the truly powerful couldn't care less about disrespect. It's the vulnerable who care. They can't afford any loss of authority, because it's their faux power.

General: Thus all the smoke and mirrors.

Director: Yes, I think that's so. Power can give you authority. But with real power, you can take that authority away and still be strong.

General: I completely agree.

Politician: Do you two really think you can stay strong with complete disrespect? I honestly don't know what kind of power could endure that for long.

General: That's because you're thinking of power over others, while Director and I are thinking of what we might call personal power.

Director: Does power over others always require authority, respect?

Politician: Yes, it does. And personal power, as you call it, gives you authority— when it's respected.

Director: Which authority is more true? Or is authority simply authority?

Politician: Authority is authority.

Director: Then, all things equal, which would you rather have—power over others or personal power?

Politician: If forced to choose? I would take personal power. But I have both, Director—as do you.

Director: I do?

Politician: Your personal power is clear. And I assume you have power over others in your role at work. You, too, General.

Director: But now something occurs to me. We're saying power over others requires authority and respect. But what if I have a boss at work who has power over my career but hasn't earned my respect at all. He has no respect but still has the power.

General: Yes, but the point is that he has power over your career, not you yourself. That's an important difference. In order for him to have power over you, you would have to have respect for him. Does that make sense?

Director: I think it does.

Politician: Sure, but not many people would make that distinction, would separate career from self.

Director: Do you?

Politician: I've never thought about it before.

General: Which means you don't. Who has power over you? Who is your authority?

Politician: The People.

General: Do you truly have respect for them?

Politician: I truly do. If I didn't, how could I respect myself?

Director: Respect yourself, yes. But we can be our own authority, right?

Politician: In the sense of blessing our thoughts and deeds, as we said? It's a very difficult thing.

Director: Why?

Politician: Because there are so many other authorities and 'authorities' clamoring around us. It's hard to focus.

Director: But if we focus, we can respect ourselves?

Politician: Of course we can respect ourselves.

Director: But if I say we can be our own authority, it sounds a little harder?

Politician: Yes, I suppose that's true.

General: It's a little... frightening.

Director: Frightening, General?

Politician: I know why he says that. It's because we take full responsibility for what happens to us.

Director: Even if it's not our fault?

Politician: We should have foreseen what would happen, our fault or not, and avoided it. Full responsibility.

Director: So if you lose an election or an important vote, it's all on you.

Politician: Yes.

Director: No excuses.

Politician: No excuses.

General: This is all true. But we have to note that we can be our own authorities yet still be subject to higher authority.

Politician: Of course. I am my own authority but the People have authority over me. There's no contradiction there. I choose to respect the authority of the People while respecting my own.

Director: And if you choose one day not to respect the People?

Politician: It would be hard to respect myself.

Director: Because you respected them so long? Because your life is so tied up with them?

Politician: Yes, but you take it a little too far. I wouldn't say my life is 'tied up' with them.

Director: You're free of any ties?

Politician: I could walk away tomorrow.

Director: That takes money.

Politician: I have money. You've seen my watch.

Director: Do you think at least part of your self-respect comes from having money?

Politician: If it does it's because of how I use that money. It's not the having. It's the use.

Director: You're right to emphasize that. And if you had less money, it would still be the use?

Politician: Of course. It's always the use.

Director: So you don't respect those who make poor use of their money.

Politician: All things equal? I don't.

Director: Money can have power but no authority.

Politician: Absolutely.

Director: But that's not enough for some.

Politician: No, it isn't.

Director: If they had authority alone, would that be enough?

Politician: The only 'enough' is having money and authority and power.

Director: A particular kind of power?

Politician: What do you mean?

Director: Well, you could have a powerful physique. That's power, isn't it?

Politician: Sure.

Director: Could you be happy with a powerful physique but no money or authority?

Politician: Do you have overall good health?

Director: Excellent health.

Politician: Then you could be happy.

General: So what are we saying? If you're not healthy and strong you can't be happy unless you pursue power, money, and authority?

Politician: No, of course not. But the funny thing is, people are all too ready to grant authority to those with health and strength. It doesn't have to be formal authority, but they tend to give them respect.

General: That's true.

Director: What should people respect?

Politician: Intellect.

General: Evil geniuses have intellect. We should respect character.

Politician: Evil geniuses have character—bad character.

General: We should respect good character.

Director: What makes a character good?

General: Many things.

Politician: Pick two.

General: Honesty and courage.

Director: Those things are hard to beat.

Politician: Are you implying I'm trying to beat them?

Director: I'm implying you'd like to one-up the general.

Politician: Well, you're wrong. I agree with the general. But I do wonder which one he'd choose if he could only have one.

General: You want my honest answer?

Politician: What else?

General: Courage.

Politician: Interesting! But, you know, evil geniuses can have courage.

General: Yes, yes. I know, and I knew you'd bring that up.

Director: Why is courage more important than honesty?

General: I can't help but think of old Odysseus. He was as wily as they come. Not always honest. But brave. And his bravery saw him through.

Politician: But his main characteristic was his wiliness—his intellect.

General: Wiles and intellect aren't the same.

Director: It's true. I know a math genius, internationally renowned, who doesn't have a single wile in him. Wiliness is something more than raw intellect.

General: It's how you use the intellect you have.

Director: Does wiliness give you authority?

Politician: You can use your wiles to weasel your way into authority. But you have to be careful.

Director: Why?

Politician: Because who respects wiles when they're known?

Director: Wiliness and secrecy go together? General?

General: I think they must. After all, if you're known by one and all to be wily, people will be on their guard around you.

Politician: In other words, the wily aren't known to have good character.

General: Yes, I think that's true.

Director: But we seem to be suggesting wiliness does in fact make for good character. After all, Odysseus is a hero, a sort of authority on doing what has to be done however it has to be done.

Politician: Getting things done gives you authority.

General: Well, that's true. Maybe wiliness is a neutral trait, neither good nor bad. It can be used for good or bad ends, and that's the difference.

Director: Then why the secrecy? But tell us. Do you consider yourself a wily general?

General: I never really have.

Politician: Maybe you should explore the possibility.

General: Maybe I should.

28

Politician: Honesty isn't the thing. It's honesty to whom. If you're dishonest with everyone, that's a problem. But if you're honest with your friends and dishonest with your enemies, that's the way. Everyone respects that.

Director: And that gives you authority as... what?

Politician: A useful man. The useful always have a natural sort of authority.

Director: So if you're a useful man with health and strength, you will have a significant amount of natural authority.

Politician: Yes, of course.

Director: And if you're a useful man with health and strength and power and money you'll have even more authority.

Politician: Yes you will.

Director: And if you cap it all off with formal authority? Say, a role in the House?

Politician: You have all the authority there is—when coupled with a high degree of intellect and wiles.

Director: General, I think we've found our man.

General: I'm inclined to agree. Though if we put him on a training regimen with me I think we can increase his health and strength. Still, he's not in bad shape for a civilian.

Politician: I'll take you up on the offer.

Director: Yes, that sounds good. But it occurs to me we're forgetting something that contributes to authority.

Politician: What?

Director: Knowledge.

Politician: Oh, of course. That's so obvious it goes without saying.

Director: What kind of knowledge do you have?

Politician: Two basic kinds. First, knowledge of my voters. Second, knowledge of the House.

General: What about knowledge of the issues?

Politician: I'll let you in on a secret. Knowledge of the issues comes through knowledge of the voters and knowledge of the House.

Director: Knowledge of what's desired and knowledge of what's possible?

Politician: Precisely. And yes, of course, I need general familiarity with the issues. But there's no need to dive deep and compete with the experts. I make use of experts. I don't want to be one myself.

Director: What do you do when experts on an issue challenge your stance?

Politician: I employ other experts to fight them. Then I take the main points and put them in my quiver to shoot from my bow as needed.

Director: But you never argue with those beneath you, right? You tarnish your authority that way.

Politician: No, Director. I argue with my voters. And they love me for it. It shows I don't think they're beneath me. And I argue with everyone in the House, as needed.

Director: And I take it you're an expert in knowing when it's needed.

Politician: Yes, I am. I'm a true authority on this. And my peers respect me for it. That's one of the reasons they'll make me Speaker one day.

Director: So you know how not to make people resent you when you argue with them.

Politician: It's a critical skill.

Director: What's the secret?

Politician: Same as with the voters. Treat them as equals.

Director: Even if they're not equals in authority?

Politician: Especially then. They feel your authority all the more!

Director: Why?

Politician: Because it shows how comfortable you are in it. You don't need to defend it by standing on high.

Director: But is it an act?

Politician: No! Don't you know democracies train their citizens from youth on up to stand on equal footing? I only do what comes natural to me.

Director: And authority comes naturally, too?

Politician: Some of us are given a gift. What can I say?

Director: When did you first notice you had authority?

Politician: On the playground as a boy. The others always chose me as their leader.

Director: Why do you think they did?

Politician: Because I was fair and knew how to have good fun. Another reason I'll be chosen as Speaker!

Director: So when you were growing up and people asked you what you wanted to be, you said, 'The leader'?

Politician: I didn't know what I wanted to be leader of. But I knew I wanted to be a leader.

Director: And as you grew your ambitions grew?

Politician: Gradually and sometimes in leaps.

Director: What would make for a leap?

Politician: Any big accomplishment. It told me there could be more. People's reaction told me there could be more. And so my confidence grew.

General: A born leader.

Politician: Yes. I'm not embarrassed to admit it. But you, General, you're quite the leader.

General: I worked very hard to get where I am.

Director: Are you suggesting Politician didn't?

General: If he were good looking I might think that. But I'd like to hear him tell us more about why he was chosen leader as a boy.

Politician: I studied all the other boys and learned what they wanted. Then I came up with things for us to do. It took some work. Maybe not as much work as it took for you, General. But I learned to strive from an early age to keep as many happy as possible. That's what I do to this day.

Director: And the arm twisting?

Politician: A necessary evil for the greater good.

Director: But let's get back to your point. Making people happy gives you authority?

Politician: People are more inclined to give you authority when you make them happy, or happier. It's only human nature. I got this authority from my schoolyard friends and kept going until—here I am now.

Director: So you're studying your peers in the House, looking to see what they want to do. And then you'll strive to make them happy. Nothing has changed.

Politician: Nothing, except the stakes.

29

Director: Why do you think people give others authority?

Politician: They want something done they can't do on their own.

Director: So, for instance, we give the police authority to arrest, and so on, because we can't do this on our own.

Politician: Can't do it as effectively, yes.

Director: And it's the same with laws. We can't legislate on our own, or do it as effectively as the legislature can.

Politician: Right.

Director: Do you think that might change with all of the advances in communication?

Politician: Direct voting on laws? It's possible. We are having more and more referendums. Direct decision.

Director: What happens to your role if the trend accelerates?

Politician: I'll adjust. Someone has to initiate the referendums. Someone has to advocate for them. There will likely be other needs we'll discover along the way.

Director: So even big changes in how we govern ourselves won't knock you off track.

Politician: Of course not. I'll always be in a position of authority because I know how to lead.

General: Fortunately, none of that stuff will touch the military. We need a command structure, not chaos. But Politician, don't you think direct democracy will necessarily lessen your authority?

Politician: Not at all! Look at Pericles. The Athenians had direct democracy, sort of, and he held great authority over them for many, many years.

General: Don't you think our President would try to occupy that place?

Politician: Many people will try to occupy that place—and not just people from government.

General: Then why you and not them?

Politician: As I've said, I'm a natural and I'll be able to adjust to the new order of things better and more quickly. But let's be clear. I don't anticipate this will happen. I still have my sights set on the Speakership.

Director: Why won't it happen?

Politician: People want decisions made for them, on their behalf. Besides, can you imagine the People trying to negotiate a budget? Impossible for them to get anything done that works.

Director: I don't know, Politician. Congress barely gets anything done that works.

General: Ha, ha. True. The problem I see is that the People are volatile while Congress is steady. For my troops to be at their best, they need steady.

Politician: Yes. Troops need authority. And while the People are the highest authority in the land, they would lose some of their authority in a wild direct democracy.

Director: Lose it because volatility and authority don't mix?

Politician: That's right. Authority takes a steady hand.

Director: Why?

Politician: So people can organize around it.

Director: The People would organize around themselves?

Politician: No, they would organize around me!

Director: Why?

Politician: In order to hold me to my promises. Lock me in, as it were.

General: I know that locked-in feeling very well. It can be a good thing. It clears away the uncertainty and focuses you on the task.

Director: I know that feeling, too.

Politician: At work?

Director: Yes, but I was thinking more as a philosopher.

General: How do you feel it, Director?

Director: People want philosophers to be authorities. They want to lock them into their words.

Politician: And you want to change your words?

Director: If I learn I'm wrong, yes.

General: How often are you wrong?

Director: Probably as much as anyone is. But I'm usually not wrong about two things. People's characters and philosophy.

Politician: How are the two related?

Director: You're not going to believe me.

Politician: Try me.

Director: People's characters are defined by how they relate to philosophy.

Politician: That's a big claim.

General: Director, that may be how you see it. But most people don't see it that way.

Director: How do they see it?

Politician: I'll tell you how. They see it in relation to their interests. Which is exactly how you, Director, see it.

Director: There's some truth in that. How do you see it?

Politician: In relation to people's interests.

General: What does that mean?

Politician: People don't always know how to act in their own interest. But sometimes they do. I judge them according to this.

Director: Do you want people around you who know their own interest?

Politician: Absolutely.

Director: Why?

Politician: They're more reliable. I know what they want and where they'll stand. It gives me something to work with.

Director: What would you call a character like this?

Politician: Solid.

Director: And the opposite?

Politician: Weak.

30

Director: Does the same hold if their interests differ from yours?

Politician: Yes. All my best enemies—the solid ones—know their interests very, very well.

Director: That's interesting. I would have thought your best interests are in line with everyone's best interests. Do you know what I mean?

Politician: Of course I know what you mean. Half the half-baked people out there think what's in their interest is in everyone's interest. In my case, however, it happens to be true. Healthcare reform really is in everyone's interest. That's why I chose it as my cause.

Director: You might really be a statesman, Politician. But what if there are a lot of weak characters out there who don't know how to act in their interest?

Politician: All they have to do is vote, vote their interest. Is that asking too much?

Director: Yes, but they sometimes have to defend their choice. Or should they keep silent?

Politician: No, they need to speak. The more they do the better my chances.

Director: Because when word about you gets around, people can't help but like you?

Politician: Yes.

Director: Will you enlist famous people to serve the cause?

Politician: Of course! But you don't have to be famous to be effective.

Director: That's true. I once met a philosopher, a great philosopher, who shunned all public attention. He dealt with handfuls of people at a time, and won them over to the cause.

General: Healthcare's cause?

Director: No, philosophy's cause.

Politician: What is philosophy's cause?

Director: Knowing your interests and acting on them.

Politician: Yes, yes. But what interests are we talking about?

Director: The interests of the heart and mind.

Politician: I didn't know philosophy concerned itself with the heart.

Director: Heart and mind should be one. Don't you agree?

Politician: Of course I agree. But when they're one, what are they?

Director: Greater than either alone.

General: I think Director makes great sense. I try to train my troops to have heart and mind as one.

Politician: Somehow I think Director's training differs from yours.

General: How so?

Politician: Director?

Director: Here's what I think. You reason your way to your heart and find what's there. Then you reason your way back and put what you found into effect.

Politician: What if in your heart you find rot?

Director: You scrape it away until you get to the core.

Politician: And those who get to the core are philosophers?

Director: Yes. But then there's work to be done.

Politician: What kind of work?

Director: If there was rot, the philosopher can't help but feel sick at heart.

Politician: So how does the philosopher get better?

Director: Through a strong desire for health.

Politician: And let me guess. This desire manifests in endless reasoning.

Director: Endless, yes—but not pointless.

General: How does a philosopher learn how to reason?

Director: It sometimes takes a touch of coaching, General.

Politician: Only a touch?

Director: The philosopher has to do it on their own.

Politician: Why?

Director: That's the only way you can stand on your own two feet. Do you know of any authorities who can't stand on their own two feet?

Politician: No, authorities always stand on their own two feet.

General: Except when they're using others as crutches.

Politician: Yes, but then they're 'authorities', not authorities.

Director: You're suggesting something radical.

Politician: Oh?

Director: We obey authorities, but we don't obey 'authorities'.

Politician: What's radical in that?

Director: I suppose it depends on the 'authorities' you come across.

General: In the military you sometimes find 'authorities'. But you have to obey them nonetheless. So I'd say that you civilians, given the freedom you have, should disobey as often as you can. That way, eventually, we'll have good leadership at our head.

Director: It's our duty to disobey?

General: If it's a bad boss at work, for instance? Yes.

Politician: And if we lose our job?

General: There's always another to be found. You don't go to prison for disobeying authority. We do. So take the chance.

Politician: Oh, you paint with too broad a brush. If we disobey the police, or a judge, we'll go to prison the same as you.

Director: I understand the authority of the police. But what's the authority of a judge?

Politician: You know full well. The judge is a guardian of the law. Her or his interpretation counts.

Director: We can interpret the law?

Politician: We? Ha, ha. At our peril, yes.

Director: But doesn't the legislature tell us what the law is?

Politician: It's not quite that simple, but yes.

Director: Why isn't it that simple?

Politician: Because laws are often made ambiguous, intentionally so.

Director: Why?

Politician: To pass responsibility on to the judge.

Director: So a judge judges two things—the facts and the law?

Politician: Yes.

Director: That gives a judge a lot of power, no?

Politician: It goes nicely with his or her be-robed authority.

General: I've always wondered why judges have to wear robes.

Politician: It emphasizes their supremacy.

Director: So judges have more authority than other government employees?

Politician: Government employees? Ha! While it's true, the judges I know rarely think of themselves like that. No, they are something higher.

Director: The highest in the land?

Politician: Well, we are a nation of laws. Judges judge the law, overturning some, and reinterpreting others. I'd say they are the highest in the land.

Director: And if they overturn your healthcare reform?

Politician: They do so at their peril.

Director: How so?

Politician: Their authority lasts only so long as they don't go too much against the People's will. My law will be directly in the People's interest. The Court would do well not to shoot it down.

Director: And they'll know this.

Politician: Of course they will! After all, judges are politicians, too—though sometimes they don't know it.

Director: Why don't they know it?

Politician: The ones who are chosen for life often don't know. The ones who run for election every few years? They know it all too well.

General: Should all judges run for election?

Politician: I think they should.

Director: What's the advantage in not running for election?

Politician: You get to believe you're above politics.

Director: Is anyone above politics?

Politician: No.

General: Not even me?

Politician: You're something of a strange exception. You're more beside politics than above or below it.

General: And yet I answer to civilians. That makes me below. No?

Director: I think Politician is saying you have an authority that puts you on level ground with politicians, even though you answer to them.

Politician: Yes, politicians know to only go so far.

Director: Why do you think that is?

Politician: They respect the authority of the military. And, also, they're afraid.

General: Afraid of what?

Politician: Your real authority versus their often... often....

Director: Sham authority?

Politician: Yes, sham authority. So whenever you see a politician kissing up to the military, there's some reason to suspect their authority is a sham.

Director: True authority does nothing more than respect true authority.

Politician: Yes, exactly so.

Director: How do we show our respect?

Politician: Sometimes only with a silent nod.

Director: How else?

Politician: By listening closely.

Director: And then acting on what we hear?

Politician: If it's within our power, yes.

Director: Can you respect someone with lesser power?

Politician: Of course you can.

Director: Can you give an example?

Politician: Many politicians have less power than I. I respect them, still.

Director: And what about the voters?

Politician: What about them?

Director: They have more power than you.

Politician: Ha, ha. Yes, it's true. And I respect them for it.

Director: Who don't you respect?

Politician: Those of weak character. Frauds. People who play both sides against the middle.

Director: What does that mean?

Politician: You play everyone for your own advantage.

Director: Shouldn't we play for our advantage?

Politician: Yes, but not at the expense of others.

Director: We should play for the benefit of others?

Politician: That's what a good politician does. How about a philosopher?

Director: Philosophers don't play. At least not in that sense.

Politician: How do they play?

Director: One side at a time, looking for truth. If the sides have truth and the middle doesn't? Then I think philosophy will play both sides against the middle.

General: You turned that on its head rather nicely.

Director: Thanks. But I think I turned it right side up.

31

Director: Politician, if authority should be for the benefit of others, which others will they be?

Politician: Like I said, everyone will benefit from healthcare reform.

Director: Yes, but that's the unusual case. Aren't there many times when only some will benefit? What then?

Politician: That's normal politics. I don't engage in normal politics.

Director: But how would you advise those who do?

Politician: I wouldn't.

Director: Oh, come on. Not everyone can be you.

General: He has a point, Politician.

Politician: Alright. All I can say is that true politics is about the greatest good for the greatest number.

Director: The greatest number? And what about the few?

Politician: Do you know what a bell curve is?

Director: I do.

Politician: Those at the bottom could use some help. But those at the top? They can take care of themselves.

General: How are you so sure? I've seen suicides among soldiers at the top.

Politician: Okay, the top isn't the easiest place to be. Since I'm at the top, I played it down.

Director: Have you ever contemplated suicide, Politician?

Politician: Have you?

Director: Of course I have. I try to contemplate all.

Politician: But you weren't serious.

Director: No, I was very serious. But I decided against it.

Politician: Why?

Director: There's probably a lot more to life than I've seen so far. And I want to serve the cause.

Politician: Philosophy. So philosophy keeps you alive?

Director: Somehow I live. Somehow philosophy exists. Together we are one.

General: I still don't know what philosophy is.

Politician: It gives hopeless drifters purpose.

Director: No, that's not it. It gives purpose, yes. But more often than not it gives a different purpose to those already strong with purpose.

Politician: Philosophy swaps purpose for purpose?

Director: Oftentimes? Yes.

Politician: What kind of purposes?

Director: Political purpose for philosophy.

Politician: Why are the two akin?

Director: Because philosophy asks what the political is.

Politician: And what is it?

Director: In a democracy? Service of the many—or the majority, if you like.

Politician: And philosophy serves no master?

Director: None.

Politician: And that's its appeal. Well, General, what do you think? Should we all become philosophers and serve no master?

General: I'm rather in the habit of service. Aren't you?

Politician: It's true. I am. Maybe we should recruit Director to the cause.

Director: The only master I serve, in a sense, is the cause of philosophy.

Politician: In a sense, sure. But what is the cause of philosophy?

Director: I can't tell you its origins, because they're very obscure. But I can tell you that philosophy attempts to correct the mistakes of the political.

Politician: Ha! What mistakes?

Director: Giving value to things that don't deserve to be valued.

Politician: What kinds of things?

General: I'll tell you. The things you promote in order to be elected.

Politician: Director, is that what you mean?

Director: I couldn't have said it better myself.

Politician: But how do I 'promote'?

General: I'll answer again. You flatter.

Politician: Oh, is that so bad?

General: If you're a truth loving philosopher, it is.

Politician: Then why don't you become a philosopher? You love truth.

General: Maybe I will. Director, will philosophy have me?

Director: The true question is whether you will have philosophy.

General: I will.

Politician: So now it's two on one.

Director: Will you have philosophy?

Politician: No thank you. I have my hands full as it is.

General: But philosophy can lighten the load.

Politician: That's what makes me distrust it, my friend.

General: Director, am I wrong in this?

Director: Philosophy gets rid of unnecessary beliefs. So, I'd say you're right.

Politician: Name an unnecessary belief.

Director: If I don't get elected the world will end.

General: If I don't get promoted the world will end. Yes, an unnecessary belief. The world won't end.

Politician: Easy to say for someone at your level.

General: Still, I am going to submit myself to the authority of philosophy.

Politician: You'll submit yourself to Director?

General: No! And no offense, Director.

Director: None taken.

General: I'm going to read philosophy and study the world through its light.

Politician: Why not study through your own light?

General: Honestly? I'm lacking in this. But philosophy won't be a crutch or a substitute. It will simply be a supplement, an aid.

Politician: Director, is that what it is to you?

General: It doesn't matter what it is to him. That's what it is to me.

Politician: Well, alright. Take your philosophy vitamins, General. And we'll see what it gets you.

32

General: Philosophy will be good for me, in part, because authority should always stretch its mind.

Director: Why especially authority?

General: Because authority tends to contract the mind.

Director: Why do you think that is?

Politician: I'll tell you why. It's because the authority you have always has you in its grip. But that's what you think, General. As for me, I have more of a grip on it than it has on me.

Director: How do you manage that?

Politician: I let my mind roam free.

Director: Except when you have to concentrate on the task at hand?

Politician: Naturally.

General: But there's always a task at hand!

Politician: No, General. There isn't. I know when my day's work is done. And when it is, I know how to relax.

Director: That sounds pretty good, General.

General: He doesn't have my job.

Politician: If your job won't allow for that, I don't want it. In fact, I'd like to find a way to change it.

General: How, by having me delegate authority?

Politician: Why not?

General: To whom? My staff is as overwhelmed as I am.

Politician: Maybe you need more staff.

General: And where will the budget come from for that?

Politician: There are ways.

General: I'd rather the money went to improving the lives of the troops.

Politician: Well, I can't help those who won't help themselves. Director, would you take more staff?

Director: Gladly. But that's not yours to give.

Politician: I know people everywhere. I'm sure someone wouldn't mind doing me a favor.

General: Are you overwhelmed at work, Director?

Director: No, I wouldn't say that. Busy, sometimes very busy. But not overwhelmed.

General: Then why would you take the extra staff?

Director: Because I know people who would know what to do with the job I'd give them.

Politician: What would they do?

Director: Help make our company a more humane place.

Politician: Ha! Then they should come work for me and make Congress more humane!

Director: If you'd have them, I'd rather they go to you.

Politician: Why, so you can have people in power?

Director: Not exactly. It's because I think Congress is the bigger mess.

Politician: I don't know your company, but you're probably right. Here, take my card. Send me their profiles. No promises, and no favors expected in return. If they look good, we'll give them a call. Same as with anyone else.

Director: Just promise me one thing.

Politician: What's that?

Director: Call them if they look interesting, not 'good'.

Politician: Ha, ha. Agreed.

General: Director, what did you mean by making things more humane?

Director: It involves a subtle shift in focus. Or maybe it's not so subtle. Anyway, it means emphasizing individuals over corporations, or governments, or armies.

General: Armies can't afford that. We have to act as one.

Politician: Yes, yes. But we live in a country of individuals. I don't see the harm.

General: We're individuals in the military, too—but we know our limits.

Politician: Trust me, Director's friends will know their limits with me.

Director: They might surprise you.

Politician: How so?

Director: They might help expand your limits, make you into a better politician.

Politician: If they can do that, they're more than welcome!

Director: General, I'd offer some to you but I understand you may not have the same hiring flexibility.

General: You might be surprised at what kind of consultants we can employ. Send some profiles my way. But how many people like this do you know?

Director: It depends on the role. Maybe a dozen?

General: How do you know them?

Director: They used to work for me.

Politician: Why don't they work for you anymore?

Director: I think of my department as a school. People come in, stay for a while, and then they move on—as it should be.

Politician: Some say the sign of a good leader is that people stay with them for a long time.

Director: If they are learning for that whole time, good. But somehow I think that's not always the case.

General: Learning what?

Director: About life.

General: I agree with you on this. To learn more, we often have to move on.

Politician: I can see the point in that. You'll never develop your own authority in the shadow of another.

General: You can be an authority to your boss on what you know and do. In fact, I want all of my staff to be an authority to me and others on the team. I want to count on them.

Director: That's an excellent point. I, too, like authorities on my team.

Politician: You two are talking about subject matter expertise. That's not the kind of authority I mean.

Director: What do you mean?

Politician: Leadership.

Director: I give my team project leadership roles all the time.

General: Yes, I do, too. They certainly have authority within their sphere. And who of us doesn't operate within a sphere?

Politician: Director?

Director: Yes, Politician?

Politician: Do you operate within a sphere?

Director: Sometimes I feel like I'm within a cube. And you? A sphere?

Politician: I roam free.

General: Free while wearing the voters' leash! Ha, ha!

Politician: You have your own leash, I might add.

General: I never said I didn't. Director, what's your leash? We all have one.

Director: You won't believe me.

Politician: Oh, don't play shy.

Director: Philosophy holds my leash.

Politician: You're so tiresome.

Director: But it's true! Every time I do something out of line she tugs and I come back from my error.

General: I wish someone would do that for me.

Politician: So, Director, philosophy is your authority.

Director: Well....

General: What is your authority? You, yourself?

Director: To some degree. But how could I have forgotten?

Politician: What are you talking about?

Director: I have a job, with a boss. He has authority over me.

General: Yes, of course. But philosophy is something else.

Director: True.

General: It's a personal standard you hold yourself to. The best of us have such standards, something above and beyond the normal call of duty.

Politician: What's your standard above and beyond?

General: Well, I'll tell you. Since I was a boy, anytime something went wrong I asked myself what I could have done to prevent it. This was even for things I wasn't directly responsible for. It became a habit. And I think this habit led me to where I am today. We share this way of looking at things.

Politician: Yes. But I have something else.

Director: Oh?

Politician: I truly serve the People. I don't just serve them in order to get their votes. I serve them because I believe I'm serving their best interest. That's my something more. But tell us more about philosophy, Director— philosophy and your job.

Director: It's very simple. If philosophy and work come in conflict, philosophy must win. It's as I said concerning prudence. That's all.

General: What would philosophy and work come in conflict over?

Director: Life.

Politician: So philosophers go around telling people about life?

Director: Only when they're sure.

Politician: How sure are you about life?

Director: Certain things in life? I'm sure.

Politician: What things?

Director: It doesn't work like that.

Politician: Why not?

Director: It has to come up naturally, or else it's no good.

Politician: If something comes up naturally tonight, you'd tell us?

Director: Of course.

Politician: Good. So let's talk about life. Who lives life to the fullest?

General: The one with most courage.

Director: I agree.

Politician: I thought for sure you'd disagree!

Director: Why? Don't you know philosophers exercise great courage?

Politician: In taking the little chances they take?

Director: Yes, of course.

Politician: I don't believe it. I think the chances you take are when the odds are good.

Director: Good that there might be success, yes. But maybe not so good concerning the consequences.

Politician: You can have success and bad consequences at once?

Director: Not so much at once. The success, if it comes, will come over time. But the consequences tend to come more quickly.

General: Why is that?

Director: Because no one can change their habits of mind at once.

Politician: What do you mean?

Director: The philosopher challenges bad habits. These habits react almost at once.

Politician: Then I don't see why you do it.

General: He's playing the long game.

Director: I am. But I play a short one, too.

Politician: Let me guess. You enjoy these conversations. Look at him smirk!

Director: I'm smiling because you're laying the groundwork to say that what I do takes no courage. Who needs courage if the work is pleasant?

General: I know it takes courage to say hard things. It's hard to speak truth to a friend.

Politician: But easy to speak to bosses you despise?

Director: When I despise I don't speak, unless in necessary defense. But I rarely despise.

Politician: Then you can't know human nature very well!

General: Who do you despise?

Politician: Politicians who don't hold themselves to my standard. And you?

General: Careerists. Director?

Director: People who know philosophy in their bones but choose to walk away. Wait. I'm not so sure about that. I guess I despise people who try to control others' thoughts. And if they know philosophy but still try to control? Then I really despise.

Politician: Is this the first time you're thinking this through?

Director: Yes, it is. I haven't given much thought to whom I despise. So, thanks.

General: He really learned something new.

Politician: Maybe. But, Director, are you saying there have been philosophers, true philosophers, who have tried to control what people think? Mental architecture, as it were?

Director: It's complicated, but I think the answer is yes.

General: How can you control people's thoughts?

Director: Think of many of the communist regimes. They try to control people's thoughts. Think of any marketing agency in a free country. They try to control people's thoughts.

Politician: Now you're going too far. There's all the difference in the world between Beijing and Madison Ave.

Director: Of course there is. But the point is that philosophers have made use of their abilities to steer people a certain way. Look at all the space in Plato's works dedicated to the soul. Did Plato even believe in the soul?

General: If he didn't, why would he write about it?

Politician: Because he wanted the unwashed to believe in soul.

General: Why?

Politician: Maybe he felt they'd be more docile that way.

Director: Or maybe it was just a whim.

Politician: That's some whim.

General: He must have wanted fame. That seems most likely to me. And he knew what people wanted to hear.

Director: Certain people, yes.

Politician: And certain people are key.

33

General: Who would be the key people today, and what kind of steering is likely to work with them?

Director: I'm not Plato enough to say.

Politician: You're a key person, General. And Director is cautiously steering you toward philosophy.

General: What's wrong with knowing things about life?

Politician: If that's all philosophy is, there's nothing wrong with that.

Director: But you think philosophy is something more.

Politician: I'm not the one who thinks it. You do.

Director: What more do I think?

Politician: That philosophy is the highest authority there is.

Director: I don't think that. You have my word.

Politician: Why isn't it?

Director: Because authority, all authority, in its heart—wants to be obeyed. Philosophy doesn't want to be obeyed. Therefore, it can't be an authority.

Politician: Is that your final, definitive statement? You who are on Philosophy's leash?

Director: Until I learn better? Yes.

Politician: He hedges even now.

Director: Why do you call honesty a hedge? Do you have to speak in absolutes in order to be honest?

General: He's got you there.

Politician: Do you think I make use of absolutes?

Director: Your People is an absolute. Isn't it?

Politician: You mean, 'Aren't they?'

Director: It, they—what difference does it make? You know full well what I'm talking about. Or do you prefer to slip away into arguments about grammar?

General: Easy, Director. Let's have another drink.

Politician: Oh, he's calm and gentle in what he says, and means no harm. The People are my absolute. But we all need absolutes. Philosophy is yours.

Director: But my absolute, if that's what it is, is without authority. Yours may well turn out to be the greatest authority there has ever been.

Politician: More reason for me to strive to lead them.

Director: So you can be the greatest statesman there ever was?

Politician: One of them. I simply want to take my proper place.

General: How do you know it's your place?

Politician: Truthfully? I'm doing all this in order to find out. It's something I now believe. I want one day to know.

Director: Those are fair words. They make me want you to succeed.

Politician: Thank you. But, General, the People are your absolute, too.

General: The People and the Nation, yes. This is the greatest authority there has ever been, no question. I serve with pride.

Director: Do they serve you?

General: What do you mean?

Director: I mean, Politician gets voted in every couple of years. The People, they serve him. And you've been promoted, so I suppose I know the answer to my own question.

General: Yes, but the People didn't promote me.

Director: Ah, I should have said the Nation did.

General: Yes, of course. The military is an important part of the Nation, headed by the President, who serves the People. So, I guess it's all one. The People promoted me. What's the point?

Director: Nothing really, I was just wondering about the difference between you and Politician in your relations to authority.

General: We both serve.

Director: That you do. How about my service?

General: To your company? Every company is an important part of the nation, so I would say you serve, too.

Politician: And with distinction, I'm sure.

Director: I'll be honest. I don't strive to serve as much as you two do. But maybe that's because you have the worthier cause.

General: I'd be lying if I said I didn't notice selfish tendencies in many companies. Self-service, simply, isn't service in the noble sense.

Director: I can tell you, there's not a lot of nobility in my company, with exceptions here and there.

Politician: You should get those exceptions onto your team.

Director: I would if I could, but they're beyond my reach.

General: Why? You run operations in an operations consulting firm.

Director: Yes, but they do what I did today. This was an exception for me. They have it as their rule.

General: Are they your peers?

Director: Yes.

Politician: Ha! You want your peers to be your subordinates! Who wants authority now?

Director: I think it would be good for them.

Politician: I'm sure you do.

General: How?

Director: I'd show them that work is about more than striving to get ahead.

Politician: What's it about?

Director: Humanity.

Politician: There you go again! But you may be right. After all, who are the People I serve if not humanity itself?

General: Aren't our People exceptional? That would make them a subset of humanity.

Director: So which is it, Politician? Do you serve all of humanity or the exceptional?

Politician: Maybe the exceptional are humanity itself.

General: Oh, you don't mean that. Haven't you ever traveled abroad?

Politician: Of course I have. And no, I don't really mean that.

Director: So you serve a portion of humanity.

Politician: You know I do. And I take it philosophy serves all of humanity?

Director: It can. But it serves the exceptional first.

Politician: Ha! Are you serious?

Director: I couldn't be more serious.

Politician: Why the exceptional first?

Director: Because more is at stake.

34

Politician: At stake for whom?

Director: All of humanity. Or don't you agree?

Politician: You're a funny one. You're trying to tempt me to think of myself as a statesman for all of humanity.

Director: Are you tempted?

Politician: Yes!

Director: So what do you have to do?

Politician: Align the interests of the People with the interests of the rest of the world. But I don't think it's possible.

Director: Well, keep it in mind as you go. And if you see any opportunities, you'll know what to do.

Politician: That's it? That's your grand teaching on the matter?

Director: Easy to say, hard to do.

General: Very hard to do.

Politician: Especially for you. You always need an enemy to justify yourself.

General: Fortunately, enemies aren't in short supply.

Politician: Do you think we make them to keep you around? Oh, I'm just kidding!

General: Sometimes I wonder. But it stops at that.

Politician: I'm sorry. We all know the bad guys started it all. Thank you for your service.

Director: I think Politician is getting a little drunk.

General: Oh, it's alright. I've heard much worse than a little light sarcasm—from my own son. And I know Politician doesn't really mean all the things he says. Or he means them if you strip away the tone. The bad guys did start it. And I believe he sincerely thanks me for my service.

Politician: Yes, I mean it sincerely even though I like to tease. But tell me what else I mean.

General: I think you mean to serve the People well. And I think you'd like to serve all people well. But you can't, and you know it. This is a great frustration. You want your authority to know no bounds. I only worry what will happen if your discontent grows too great.

Politician: You think I'd turn?

General: Against the People? No. But you might turn against yourself.

Politician: Director?

Director: General put it well. So no matter what, Politician—don't turn against yourself.

Politician: And if I do?

Director: The People will suffer for it.

Politician: Now you're playing on my vanity.

Director: You're a statesman in the making. I have no doubt. Whether you succeed or not largely depends on how you treat yourself.

Politician: You really don't think it's self-serving to say if I treat myself well, I treat the people well?

Director: Of course it is. But you can't treat the people well unless you treat yourself well.

Politician: What does it mean to treat myself well?

Director: To never despair.

Politician: How do you know I'm at risk for despair?

Director: Your sort always is. Hazarding all on a vote? That might drive me to despair!

Politician: Ha, ha. You have a point. But if I ever lose....

Director: I know. It's unthinkable. So think about it. Break that mental block that says failure is not an option.

General: That's not a good block to break.

Director: Maybe not for you. But for Politician? I think it is.

Politician: Why for me but not him?

Director: If General fails, people die—and the Nation is at risk. If you fail, a bunch of your supporters will be disappointed.

Politician: It's not as simple as that.

Director: How simple is it?

Politician: It's about who I am.

Director: Who are you? God's gift to the People?

General: Director....

Politician: No, he has a point. But it's the opposite. The People are God's gift to me. They need to be led. And I will lead them.

Director: That sounds better, I think. But suppose the gift is taken away. What will you do?

Politician: Find a way to get it back.

Director: That definitely sounds better. It's not all or nothing on one throw. You have many possible approaches here.

Politician: Not as many as you might think.

Director: But more than one?

Politician: I suppose.

General: It's hard for him even to think it.

Director: Politician, you've been bent to your task a long while. It's good you're looking up and embracing the possible.

Politician: The possible. The art of the possible. Politics.

Director: Yes. And unless you embrace that art fully, you can't be the consummate politician.

Politician: Failure is possible.

Director: It has to be.

Politician: Why?

Director: Because if not, you're not truly taking risks. And risks are what bring us true success.

General: That's an excellent point. But maybe Politician doesn't want real risks. Maybe he wants a sure thing.

Politician: No, I don't want that. There's no such thing. To want a sure thing is folly. I have two major risks. One, I won't get re-elected. Two, my legislation won't pass.

Director: What if your legislation passes but you don't get re-elected?

Politician: I could live with that.

Director: And if you get re-elected but your legislation doesn't pass?

Politician: Then I fail to see the point of being elected.

Director: Election is the means; the legislation is the end.

Politician: Yes.

Director: What if you work toward passing the legislation from outside of the House?

Politician: No, I want my name on it.

Director: That's an absolute?

Politician: That's an absolute.

Director: You know that absolute will constrain you, make you less flexible.

Politician: I'm extremely flexible. But even the most flexible person in the world needs at least one absolute. Otherwise, what are they?

Director: So you're saying you'll have no hard and fast rules except for this one ambition?

Politician: This ambition is my only rule. Yes. And if you tell the voters, I'll deny it.

Director: Now you've both said things you want to deny.

Politician: I don't want to deny it, but I will.

General: And I was speaking in general terms about our youth.

Director: You said we're doomed.

General: And maybe we are.

Director: A lot of youth come up through your ranks.

General: You think I can stem the tide?

Director: You can try.

General: How?

Director: By showing them your example. Get out among them more.

General: I would, but I'm bogged down in politics, budgets—headaches.

Director: Get out into the fresh air with your troops. Let Politician help you here.

Politician: I can cut down on some of your load.

General: You would do this?

Politician: Consider it done.

General: If you can do this, you don't know how grateful I'd be. I hate that stuff.

Politician: Like I said, consider it done. But don't complain if another general steps onto center stage.

General: They can have it. I'd rather be with the troops. The youth. Our future.

Politician: So, Director, while General deals in the thousands, you'll have your dozen or so.

Director: To each his own. And you, you'll have the nation. Who will have the greater authority?

General: Director will. His authority won't be dilute.

Politician: It doesn't work that way. Authority grows with numbers.

Director: So you will have the greatest authority.

Politician: I think that's fair to say.

Director: Next, perhaps, to the President?

Politician: You're unbelievable. Now you're trying to suggest I run for President.

Director: General, did you hear me suggest that?

General: No, I think Politician had it in mind.

Politician: To get things done I need to stay in the House. That's my strength.

Director: Okay. You would know best. Maybe after your legislation passes you could consider a run.

Politician: Maybe. But just to have something to do.

General: Ha! You'd be the highest authority in the land!

Politician: No, the nine Justices are.

Director: I've always marveled that people respect the Court's rulings the way they do.

Politician: There are two reasons for that. The rulings are backed by force. And we believe in the rule of law.

Director: Who believes most?

Politician: The lawyers.

Director: Ah, the secular priests of our nation.

General: Why do you say that?

Director: Priests intermediate with the gods. Lawyers intermediate with the laws. We swapped the gods for the laws. We lost the priests and gained... lawyers.

35

General: I never looked at it that way before.

Politician: It only goes to remind us that law should be simple. There is no need for lawyers then. My laws will be simple and clean.

General: Why did lawyers ever even come about?

Politician: Corruption is my guess. Laws were made to favor certain people and needed to be explained away.

Director: Some of the first lawyers were advocates who spoke on behalf of other people in court.

General: Politician, do you have a problem with those who represent others?

Politician: Like me? Ha, ha. But I admit the situation is problematic.

Director: How so?

Politician: There's one simple question that says it all. 'Why can't people speak for themselves?' I'm aware of what this means.

Director: What does it mean?

Politician: If people truly need me, that means they're inarticulate sods. If they don't need me, why am I here?

General: You're being too hard on the inarticulate. Most of them have good hearts. They just don't know how to put what they feel into words. Surely you know that.

Politician: That's what I like to believe.

Director: Does it matter how much or little people need you?

Politician: Doesn't it?

Director: They want healthcare. You might be able to give it to them. They need you at least to that extent. Do you really need more?

Politician: You're colder than I thought.

Director: Politics is a cold-headed game.

Politician: True. I'm letting emotions get in the way, aren't I?

Director: If you long for people to need you in some profound or spiritual way, I'd say yes. Do you long like that?

Politician: I don't. But it's a temptation, a danger. That I can see.

Director: Then be sure to avoid it.

Politician: I will.

General: But what of your talk about going beyond using them for their votes?

Politician: I am going beyond. I'm using their votes to give them what they want. Nothing has changed. Director just pointed out something to guard against.

General: Spell out for me what you're guarding against.

Politician: Tying my self-worth to their need for me. It's a trap. Some of the best fall for it.

General: I want my troops to need me. Have I fallen into the trap?

Politician: Your relationship to your troops is very different than mine to the voters. The troops are truly in your care. Not so with the electorate. They're independent of me. In fact, I'm dependent on them!

General: Well, I depend on the troops, of course.

Politician: Yes, of course. But you take my point?

General: I do. So what should I guard against?

Politician: I'm not sure. I guess letting all your authority go to your head. It's happened with generals before.

General: I'm well aware. Director, is there anything else I should guard against?

Director: Thinking you can't do good from outside.

General: Outside the military? Politics?

Director: No, I mean really outside.

Politician: What's outside politics?

Director: I don't know. But General might find out.

Politician: The Justices think they're outside politics.

Director: Is that what they think? Or is that what they say?

Politician: Some of them really believe it.

General: So you're saying I need something to believe? Something apart from it all?

Politician: I don't think it would hurt.

General: And neither of you have any idea what?

Politician: I don't have anything.

Director: I can make a recommendation.

General: Please.

Director: As you search, just keep your mind open and have no preconceptions.

General: That's always good advice. But what am I searching for?

Director: You'll know when you find it. That's all I can say.

General: Well, that's not much to go by. But I take it in the spirit in which it was intended.

Politician: It might be something like my ambition. Maybe you'll find an ambition.

General: You don't become a general without ambition, Politician.

Politician: Yes, yes. But an ambition for something more. Something rare. Something unique.

General: I think you think too highly of me.

Politician: No, I know your mettle. Just look, and I bet you'll find it. And, after all, I'll be there to help!

General: Yes, and I won't be shy to take your help. But I should say—I think I have a pretty good idea of your ambition now.

Politician: Oh?

General: Your ambition is to make something that is the highest authority in the land—law. And yes, I know we all know this. But there's something more. You don't want the highest authority for yourself. You want to be its creator. You want to birth this authority and let it stand on its own. Your lesser authority is just a tool, a means toward this end.

Politician: I'm glad you're catching on. Maybe you, too, can create.

General: I won't create law. That's not my thing. But who knows? Maybe I'll find something else. Maybe I'll take up... painting.

Politician: Maybe you will—in addition to something grand.

General: Sometimes just retiring sounds grand.

Politician: Ah, it's getting late and you're tired. Me? I want to die in the saddle. What about you, Director?

Director: I don't much care if I'm working a job or not when I go. But I would like to be with my friends. Do you have friends, Politician?

Politician: Aside from my colleagues, you mean? I do. But my time for them is short. It's the price I pay. But I'd like them there when I die. General?

General: I'd like to die like some of the animals do—walk off into the woods on my own and never come back.

Politician: Ah. But why are we talking about death! There's so much more life to live.

Director: There's something I wonder, Politician. Something about how to spend our lives. We all have responsibilities, no?

Politician: Yes.

Director: What do you think about this formula? The more responsibility we successfully bear, the greater the authority we have.

Politician: It's probably true. So what's the question? Should we spend our lives trying to bear more and more responsibility? That's what I do. That's what the general does. How about you? What does the philosopher say?

Director: I bear the responsibilities I must. But I don't seek to add more to them.

Politician: You'll never get ahead.

Director: Well, I think it depends. If my boss likes my work, he's likely to give me more responsibility—like this trip I'm on now.

Politician: You should exploit your luck! Press your boss for more trips.

Director: No, I'd rather be recognized for good work without thrusting myself forward.

Politician: You'll never be recognized. People will think there's something wrong with you for not pushing your way to the front. Everyone pushes.

General: That's not true. Some of us wait.

Politician: Are you waiting for something, Director?

Director: I am. For someone to recognize me for what I am.

General: We're all waiting for that. We want that full human connection. Don't you want that, Politician?

Politician: The People give me that. Do you doubt it?

General: I've never had what you have, so I honestly don't know what to think.

Director: I doubt it, Politician. But only because I, too, don't know what to think. Do you love the People?

Politician: Why do you ask?

Director: Because when people speak of a full human connection, they're usually speaking of love. Was that what you meant, General?

General: Yes. But not romantic love. Nothing soft focused and flowery. I'm talking about pure love—human to human. Have you had that Director?

Director: For fleeting moments, yes.

Politician: Why didn't it last?

Director: That's very hard to say.

Politician: Let me guess. They had too high an opinion of you, and you didn't want to be found out—so you pushed them away.

Director: If I were found out, I would have lost their love? I have to object. No, if I were found out it might well have increased the love.

Politician: And you didn't want that?

Director: You're assuming I pushed them away.

General: Then why didn't it last?

Director: Our contact didn't last. But I'm inclined to believe the love went on and on.

Politician: The world forced you apart.

General: I can understand that.

Politician: Well, I can't. That sounds like foggy headed romance to me.

Director: What can I say? There were fleeting moments.

General: Don't press him too hard on this, Politician. What he's talking about is rare and to be respected.

Politician: I suppose you'd say you're an authority on this fleeting moment stuff, Director?

Director: I'd say I am.

Politician: Have you had it more than once?

Director: I have. Have you?

Politician: I've had moments of truth. I've had seeing eye to eye. I've had that perfect touch of understanding. Does that count?

Director: That's something you should ask yourself, not General and me.

General: Politician, you didn't mention love.

Politician: Oh, of course I've had love.

Director: Did your authority play a part in the love?

Politician: The love was for what I am. And I am, no doubt, at least in part, an authority.

Director: Do you believe that the more authority you have the more love you'll have?

Politician: Let me ask you this. Who is worth loving? Someone who successfully bears great responsibility, or some lazy lout?

Director: If pressed, I'd be forced to say the lout.

Politician: Oh, be serious!

General: The idea of 'worth loving' makes no sense.

Politician: Why not?

General: Because we love who we love. And then we think the world of them. We give them worth.

Director: We gain in worth by being loved?

General: Yes, certainly.

Politician: Then we should all strive, as I do, to be loved as much as possible.

Director: Can the love of one be worth more than the love of another?

Politician: What, you mean what if an authority on love, like you, loves someone? Is it worth more than love from another? I'll leave it to General to decide.

General: Love is love. Authority has nothing to do with it.

Director: I can go along with that. Politician?

Politician: There will always be love for true authority. And I'll always be happy to have it.

36

Director: Who can argue with that? But to be clear, are you saying authority and worth are linked?

Politician: Yes, I am.

Director: Are you suggesting those without authority have no worth?

Politician: Yes. But you have to understand what I mean.

Director: Please enlighten us.

Politician: We all have responsibility for ourselves. If we bear it well, we're authorities of sorts—authorities on ourselves. Someone like that has worth.

General: But they'd have more worth if they were in your position?

Politician: It's hard to say. The position might distract them from themselves.

Director: Are you an authority on yourself?

Politician: Yes. As are you two on yourselves.

Director: What responsibilities for ourselves do we have?

Politician: We're all responsible for our success. We're all responsible for our own mistakes. We're all responsible to learn and grow.

Director: So we seek success, make mistakes along the way, and learn and grow from them.

Politician: Yes.

Director: Does it matter what kind of success we seek? Or is part of the responsibility defining success for ourselves?

Politician: It's part of the responsibility.

Director: What if my definition of success is never falling out with anyone?

Politician: You'll never get anywhere in life.

Director: Does that mean I'm not living up to my responsibility?

Politician: It does. You took the easy way out.

Director: It's irresponsible to never fall out.

Politician: I'd say it is.

Director: How do we coach someone like this, someone who never falls out, so they can have more authority over themselves?

Politician: Ask them what they believe.

Director: How does that help?

Politician: In my experience, those who don't really believe anything never stand up to others. They never have the opportunity to have a falling out.

Director: So we get them to believe something?

Politician: Don't you think it's irresponsible not to believe in anything?

Director: I don't know if 'irresponsible' is the right word. But I think there's an important point here. Authority and belief have always gone hand in hand. In fact, I'm not sure it's possible to separate the two.

General: When you separate the two you have authoritarianism.

Director: That may be. Authority for the sake of authority. But now I wonder. Do the authoritarians have well borne responsibilities?

General: Of course not.

Director: What if the authoritarians are responsible for the defense of the country and they succeed in keeping it safe?

General: I've known some of those people in my time. They didn't succeed. Others had to clean up the messes they made.

Director: They put the country at risk?

General: Absolutely.

Director: If you had the authority, would you get rid of them all?

General: In a heartbeat.

Director: Maybe that's your grand ambition.

General: Maybe so. But I'm not cut out to be President.

Politician: Maybe Secretary of Defense? You could influence the President to get rid of them all.

General: If the President chose me I'm not sure I'd refuse. But the choice isn't up to me.

Politician: But you can influence the choice.

General: How? By lobbying for the rest of my life? No thanks. If chosen, I'd serve. But that's really just up to luck.

Politician: I could start a quiet campaign. I'd love to see you succeed.

General: Thank you. But excuse me for being so blunt. What would you expect from me?

Politician: You'd certainly owe me a big favor. I don't know what it would be until the time comes. Can you live with that?

General: As long as what you ask isn't illegal, unethical, or immoral—I could live with that.

Politician: Then we have a deal. Besides, I really would like to see you succeed. It would make me feel there's something right in the world.

Director: What kind of President would you like to serve, General?

General: One with integrity.

Director: How does integrity relate to authority?

General: As far as I'm concerned? The more integrity you have the more authority.

Director: Does this differ from bearing responsibilities well?

General: That's an interesting question. I think it does. I think there are two sources of authority—bearing responsibility well and integrity.

Director: You can have integrity and not bear responsibility well?

General: Yes, sometimes we're in over our head. But we can have integrity nonetheless.

Politician: But who's going to care if you have integrity if you're floundering? Is that the kind of chief you want to serve?

General: Obviously I want to serve a chief who has full authority. But you can't cut out the moral element.

Director: Morality—integrity—gives authority. But that doesn't always mean you're right for the job.

General: That's true.

Director: But if you're right for the job and have no integrity?

General: I say you can't be right for the job.

Director: So integrity always comes first.

General: Always.

Director: And authoritarians, what of their integrity?

General: They have none.

Politician: What if they have integrity for the sake of authority?

General: Authority is the end and integrity is the means? No, that's not right. Authority must serve another end. Your authority serves the People. My authority serves the Nation. Director's authority serves his friends. Absent a good end, authority is worse than useless—it actually harms.

Politician: But integrity is still a means. Or will you tell us integrity is the end?

General: Is integrity good for its own sake? I think it is. If I had nothing but my integrity, I'd be satisfied.

Politician: I wouldn't. I'd need something more. Does that make me bad?

Director: Are you asking if it's bad to tell the truth? No, you should say what you think. But really, integrity always has a powerful effect. No?

General: It does.

Director: So it's never really integrity on its own. Consequences follow. Which means, to me, that integrity is both an end, as you say, and the means towards these consequences.

General: End and means. Yes, I think that's true. But the end comes first.

Politician: I think that's fine, even though it's putting the cart before the horse!

General: Every end is a means.

Director: And every means should be an end.

Politician: How can you say that?

Director: I try to live my life in such a way that everything I do is an end. If the end leads to other ends, that's great.

Politician: And I try to live my life in such a way that everything I do serves my one and only end. My legislation.

Director: You're taking a very real risk with your life.

Politician: Yes, I am.

General: Yes, but each and every end can be a real risk. I'm sure Director agrees.

Director: I do. Yet I marvel at how all of Politician's tributary risks join the greater flow of the risk of his life.

Politician: I suspect, Director, that it's the same with you.

Director: In a sense. But I think there's an important difference.

Politician: Do tell.

Director: You're focused on the greater risk. I stay focused on the smaller risks.

Politician: But with an eye to the greater goal.

Director: I let that goal take shape on its own from the smaller risks.

Politician: I don't believe you.

General: Why would he lie?

Politician: He doesn't want to admit how enormous a role philosophy plays in his life.

Director: Oh, but I do admit it. Philosophy is how I manage all the smaller risks.

General: Is philosophy your end?

Director: And means.

Politician: Philosophy is everything to him.

Director: Oh, I wouldn't say that. At most, philosophy is my guiding star.

Politician: You just said philosophy is your end and means! Now it's just some point of reference?

Director: I stand corrected. Philosophy is more than some point in the sky.

General: But don't downplay the role of a guiding star for those who are lost.

Politician: Are you lost, Director?

Director: If I am, I suppose I can't be much of an authority.

Politician: How would you know you're not lost?

Director: I can get to where I'm going.

Politician: But you don't know where you're going, do you?

Director: I... don't.

Politician: Ha! Some authority you are.

Director: But I find many good things along the way.

General: That's something.

Politician: Of course it's something. But it never leads anywhere.

Director: What's wrong with that?

Politician: We all need to go somewhere with our lives.

Director: I'm going somewhere.

Politician: Yes, yes—but somewhere specific.

Director: Why?

Politician: Because that's the game of life!

37

Director: But I'm not playing a game. I'm just living.

Politician: Maybe that's why you'll never attain to a higher rank than the one you have.

Director: What's wrong with being a director?

Politician: Nothing, if you don't want to become a senior director, or an associate vice president, or a vice president, or a senior vice president, or an executive vice president, or the president yourself.

Director: Depending on circumstances, I don't think I would turn any of those jobs down. But to make them the point of my life? No thanks.

Politician: Well, no one is going to offer them to you, for you to turn down or not—if you don't get moving!

Director: Seek more responsibility. Yes, you've already said. But I choose to focus on the responsibilities I already have, not grasp for more. And who knows? Maybe someone will notice I've done a good job.

General: That's what I like to see in junior officers. Doing the task at hand, and doing it well. I notice these things, Director. There must be civilians who do the same.

Director: I'm sure there are.

Politician: But you haven't found them yet. Are you even looking?

Director: How would I do that?

Politician: You network with peers and they tell you what's what.

Director: Oh, you mean I talk with friends. I do talk with friends. But nothing has come of it yet.

Politician: Your friends probably don't hold high enough rank.

Director: Some of them do. One is a president of his own company. Another is a senior vice president. But is that really the point? Can't they know 'what's what' from more lowly positions?

Politician: Maybe. But they don't have the influence to bring you in.

Director: Are you suggesting I network and make false friends who might bring me in?

Politician: There is nothing false about networking. It just means you make professional friends.

Director: Professional friends? As distinct from unprofessional friends?

General: Director, I share your distaste for this.

Politician: You'd better get over that or you'll never be Secretary of Defense. And know this. Networking is about more than landing a job. It's how you get things done.

Director: I get things done.

Politician: Yes, but I'm talking about at higher levels. It's all about networking then.

General: It's all about politics then.

Politician: Of course.

General: I'm not very well equipped for that.

Politician: Oh, don't be coy with me. You don't become a general without knowing how to politic your way through things.

Director: What does 'to politic' mean?

Politician: To work problems through with others.

Director: Oh. I know how to do that.

Politician: Yes, but part of this working through involves giving them what they want in order to get what you want.

Director: We both want to solve the problem.

General: I think Politician is saying the problem is the excuse for everyone getting what they want.

Politician: That's astute.

Director: So we want to find problems to use as the vehicles for getting what we want.

Politician: In a nutshell? Yes. And that makes us highly effective operators. Self-interest motivates us to do things that will benefit others.

General: Not if you're creating problems in your own self-interest.

Politician: Do you really think there aren't enough problems in the world? Do we really need to make more?

General: If you make them, you probably know how to solve them.

Director: Manufactured problems. But in either case, naturally occurring or manufactured, solving will increase your authority, no?

Politician: It will. It's your responsibility to solve the problem. So it's in keeping with what we said before.

General: But one authority is natural, is true; while the other is manufactured, or false.

Director: Would you say that manufactured authority is a sort of perceived authority, as opposed to true authority?

General: I would.

Politician: But, as we said, perception is reality. In other words, if someone thinks you have authority, you have authority.

General: That's a dangerous game. It's building a house of cards.

Politician: You have a point. But, again, there are plenty of very real problems for me to solve—healthcare first among others.

Director: So you have to begin by making yourself responsible for healthcare? And if so, how do you do it?

Politician: Yes, that's the first step. And how do I do it? I announce that I'm going to do it, that it's mine to do.

Director: I understand saying you're going to do it. But what do you mean by saying it's yours to do?

Politician: I'll announce that it's my responsibility, and that if I can't do it, I don't deserve to be in the House.

General: But why say all that?

Politician: Because I play best when the stakes are high.

Director: And if you win, are you the greatest authority in the land?

Politician: I don't know about 'greatest'. But I can say none would be greater.

Director: And what will you do with all that authority? Just retire once you've won?

Politician: I'll use it for other things.

General: Like a run for President?

Politician: Possibly. But I think there is other legislation that's more important.

Director: Like what?

Politician: A Constitutional Amendment.

General: For what?

Politician: Something for my friends the Senators, again. I want their terms to last two years. I want them to feel the pressure we Representatives feel. Now they have six-year terms, and that makes them comfy.

General: But then why have two separate chambers?

Politician: One day I'd merge them into one. But it's one step at a time.

Director: Why merge them? Doesn't that go against the wisdom of those who framed the system?

Politician: What kind of wisdom was that? They wanted the Senators to be less subject to the popular will. And they are. But my lodestar is the People. And I'd have them have more say.

Director: So you won't have them appointed by the House?

Politician: I'm still working all of this out.

General: But be honest, Politician. Wouldn't you like to be a Senator with the luxury of every six years?

Politician: I'm not looking for luxury. I'm looking for results. Senators can afford to drag their feet and delay. I'd rather they not.

Director: In other words, you're in a hurry.

Politician: I have a sense of urgency, if that's what you mean. People are dying every day. I'd like to stanch the wound.

Director: But which should really come first? Healthcare reform or the Constitutional Amendment?

Politician: You have a point. The Amendment should come first. It will speed the other along.

General: A Constitutional Amendment as the means to another end. You have quite the ambition.

Politician: And quite the problem to fix.

38

Director: Do Senators have more authority than Representatives?

Politician: They seem to, because they serve for more time.

Director: And there are fewer of them.

Politician: That, too.

Director: But you'd cut their authority by cutting their terms.

Politician: I would. Because now they don't get much of anything done.

Director: But do they really have more authority, whether from time served or fewer numbers?

Politician: Why do you ask?

Director: Because more authority implies more responsibility successfully borne. Is that how it is with them?

Politician: No.

Director: So numbers, time served—they don't equal authority.

Politician: Of course they don't. But the Senators act like they do.

Director: Ah, the way they act. That's what you don't like.

Politician: It's true. I don't like the way they act.

Director: You want revenge on them for slights?

Politician: Regardless of slights, and what have you—I think Senators should feel more of the force of the People's will.

Director: Why?

Politician: Then they'll know better what needs to be done.

Director: Senators were meant to be buffers against the People's will. Originally, they weren't even popularly elected.

Politician: And an Amendment fixed all that, or most of it. I'll fix the rest.

Director: Why not fix the President while you're at it? And the High Court?

Politician: Both could use a fix, the High Court especially. Can you imagine going from Justices for life to judges elected every two years?

Director: How do you think it would affect the law?

Politician: It would better serve the People's needs. Serve their needs or lose your chair.

General: What about wisdom?

Politician: Their kind of wisdom is nothing but the interests of the rich.

General: Oh that's not true. I think you're getting carried away.

Politician: Maybe I am. But do you deny that the overall tendency of our government is to favor the rich?

General: There's some truth to that. The poor don't always get a fair shake.

Director: What about your soldiers?

General: The 'shake' they get is based, for the most part, on merit.

Director: That sounds good. Would you like to see the country as one great big military camp, for the sake of great shakes?

General: No, but I would like everyone to serve if only for a year. That would teach them something of merit.

Director: Merit being responsibility borne well. So you'd teach them something about true authority.

Politician: Yes, but military skills aren't the only skills in life.

General: I know. That's why they'd only serve a year. Then they can come running back to you.

Director: Military skills, political skills. What other skills are there in life?

General: Business skills?

Politician: Yes, but I think he wants us to say philosophical skills.

Director: I don't want you to say anything other than what you think.

General: I think there are philosophical skills.

Politician: Name one.

General: Logical thought.

Politician: Oh but that's a skill for any walk of life. I want to hear about something peculiar to philosophy.

Director: How about teasing out hidden beliefs?

General: Why would philosophy do that?

Director: In order to put them to the test.

Politician: What test?

Director: To see whether they're worthy of the holder.

General: We can hold beliefs that are beneath us?

Director: Of course we can.

Politician: He's saying they're beneath us if they're untrue. So, how can we know a belief is true? After all, we believe when we don't know.

General: The belief can be true to our soul. That's how we know. Director?

Director: You put that very well. So we must know our soul well. We have a responsibility to ourselves and others to do so. And this gives us great natural authority. Yes?

General: Yes.

Politician: Suppose you have a deformed soul, and you hold a belief that fits it quite well. Is that good?

General: Of course not. You have to fix your soul then find the right belief.

Politician: How well will that go over if we make it our business to tell someone this?

General: Probably not very well.

Director: Yes, but that's not our concern.

General: What do you mean?

Director: Philosophy concerns itself with beautiful souls. It wants to bring the full beauty out.

Politician: How does it do that?

Director: By exposing the bad beliefs. And that's it. Nothing more. The other recognizes them as bad or doesn't. It's all in their hands.

Politician: And this is all in a friendly conversation?

Director: Yes. Friendly is best. Otherwise too many other things get in the way.

Politician: And you're an authority on this?

Director: I am.

Politician: What bad beliefs have we exposed tonight?

Director: Ah, the night is still young. But can I ask you a favor?

Politician: Of course.

Director: Please point out any—and I mean any—bad beliefs that I might hold, that you can see.

39

Politician: 'That you can see.' That's the thing, isn't it? It's hard to see what people believe deep down inside. It's hard when they're living, and it's infinitely harder once they're dead. I often wonder about the beliefs of statesmen long gone. Do you wonder that about philosophers?

Director: There was a time when I did. But I don't anymore.

General: I wonder what it would be like to meet generals from the past. Would we have been friends?

Politician: I wonder that, too. Surely you wonder that about your own, Director.

Director: Again, there was a time when I wondered that. But I don't anymore.

General: Because you know you would be friends?

Politician: No, it's because he knows they couldn't be friends.

Director: Why do you think that is?

Politician: Because your little corner of philosophy is only big enough for you.

Director: And you think the same holds for all philosophers?

Politician: Yes.

Director: Why doesn't it hold for politicians?

Politician: Politicians don't dwell in corners.

General: Director doesn't seem like a corner dweller to me. Look how he contributes to our conversation tonight—and he didn't even know us!

Politician: Yes, but bring another philosopher in and see what Director does.

Director: I've had conversations with philosophers.

Politician: Alone or with others?

Director: Both.

Politician: Are you friends with these philosophers?

Director: I'd say we're on friendly terms. But we have different interests, so we haven't stayed in touch.

Politician: Do you think that's of necessity?

Director: Not staying in touch? Only if it's necessary to spend your time on your interests. Is it?

General: We all spend as much time on our interests as we can.

Director: I have my doubts. I think some people don't spend as much time as they could.

General: Why do you think that is?

Director: Maybe they get caught up in niceties.

General: Niceties doesn't sound so bad. But what do you mean?

Director: Suppose I decide I need to spend lots of time courting other philosophers because they're philosophers, and only because they're philosophers. That amounts to wasteful niceties.

Politician: I know what you mean. I could spend endless time on niceties with other Congressmen. That would get me exactly nowhere.

General: What gets you somewhere?

Politician: Sticking to the point. And I'm not saying we should be rude. We just can't lose sight of the end.

Director: Who is most likely to lose sight of the end?

Politician: Those who bow down to authority, true or false.

Director: They can't tell the difference?

Politician: Some can't. Others don't care. They bow, cringe, and grovel.

Director: Do you have cringers and grovelers in your camp?

Politician: My broad camp, yes; my inner circle, never.

Director: Why not?

Politician: They can never tell me what I need to know.

Director: What do you need to know?

Politician: How much true authority I actually have.

Director: You can't know that yourself?

Politician: It's good to have mirrors.

General: That sounds vain.

Politician: I'm not looking to admire my less than handsome self. I'm looking to see the truth.

Director: What will you do with this truth?

Politician: Use it to my advantage. Serious players need to know where they're weak. I'm serious. And I want to know.

Director: Well, I'd have to know you better to say. General, you know Politician passing well. Where is he weak?

General: Where he is strong.

Director: What does that mean?

Politician: I know what it means. Jealousy. There are always those who hate true strength.

Director: What can you do with the jealous?

Politician: Some try to appease them. But what you need to do is crush them without mercy.

General: Or ignore them.

Politician: If you ignore them they only gain in strength.

Director: How do you crush them?

Politician: I see to it they never win or regain their seat.

Director: But if they do?

Politician: I see to it they never get anything done.

Director: What if they offer to vote for your legislation?

Politician: I change my tactics to secure their vote. But after the vote, I make an example of them.

General: But then why would others want to vote your way if that's what might happen to them?

Politician: A little fear goes a long way in the House.

Director: Are politicians really that weak?

Politician: Many are. Some are strong. Few are wise.

Director: What's the difference between wisdom and strength?

Politician: Both can give you authority. Wisdom can do it without strength; strength can do it without wisdom. Which do you think is better?

General: Both at once is the only true way.

Director: Strength seems fairly easy to know. But how can you recognize wisdom, Politician?

Politician: Well, what is wisdom?

Director: I think you should tell us.

Politician: Let's say it's getting what you want.

General: I don't like the sound of that.

Politician: Maybe you'll like it better if I say wisdom is helping others get what they want.

General: That does sound better. And then they can help you in turn.

Politician: Yes, but why do that dance?

General: What do you mean?

Politician: We can simply help ourselves at the start.

General: Maybe 'the dance' has to do with guarding against jealousy, or some other bad thing. I don't know. It just seems better that way. Less selfish; more humane.

Director: Is Politician's political weakness thinking he can go it alone? I know he needs to build support, gather votes, and so on. But you seem to be getting at something fundamental here, General.

Politician: I'm listening, General. Speak.

General: If you're isolated, essentially isolated, no matter how many hearts and minds you win, you'll never tap into your full strength.

Politician: What is this strength?

General: Love. I'm talking about love for your fellow women and men.

Politician: Then it all hinges on what we mean by 'fellow'. I don't believe in love for humanity, if humanity means every featherless biped. My fellow man is of a certain quality.

Director: Is that quality that he's smart enough to vote for you?

Politician: Yes, we might say that.

General: But that's the thing. That's your weakness. On the one hand, you believe every citizen is equal. On the other hand, you believe some are more equal than others.

Politician: We all believe the latter. We don't really love everyone, though some of us tell ourselves we do. We love who we love. I love many of those who vote for me. That's who I want to serve. But not them all.

Director: But you end up serving them anyway.

Politician: There's nothing to be done about that. That's the price I pay.

40

Director: I don't have to pay that price. I love who I love and serve only them.

Politician: You can't tell me you don't serve people at work you despise.

Director: I don't despise anyone at work.

Politician: Okay, I forgot we defined who you despise in a particular sense. But surely you must serve those you don't love.

Director: I make a distinction here. It's one thing to serve, and I serve my friends; it's another thing to get done what needs to get done.

General: How do you serve your friends?

Director: I put their interests almost on par with my own.

Politician: Ha! At least you're honest. General, can you do better than that?

General: If we don't help ourselves first, we can never help anyone else.

Politician: Three honest men in a hotel bar stranded during a blizzard. What other truths can we speak?

Director: Some people say, 'Dare to speak truth to authority.'

Politician: No, they say, 'Dare to speak truth to power.'

Director: I like my version better.

Politician: Why?

Director: Because power can handle the truth; authority sometimes can't.

Politician: Why can power handle the truth?

Director: Power is supple and doesn't feel harmed; authority can be rigid and feel truth as a threat.

General: I feel the truth in that.

Politician: So do I. From now on I'll speak truth to authority. And that will enhance my authority with those who like the saying!

General: It will enhance your reputation more than your authority.

Politician: A good Politician knows how to transform reputation into authority.

Director: How is it done?

Politician: You have to educate people. Show them that what underlies your reputation is a responsibility we all have to speak the truth. If I bear this responsibility well, I'll be an authority on the matter.

Director: And when you have this authority?

Politician: I'll use it to get more votes.

Director: With the electorate or in the House?

Politician: Both.

Director: Your peers would be impressed by a reputation for truth?

Politician: They're not as bad a lot as you might think. Many of them will be impressed. And the rotten ones? You just have to let them rot.

Director: Who are the authorities you'd speak truth to? One might think they're your very peers.

Politician: Yes, sure. But there's the Senate, the President, the Justices, Governors, all sorts of State and Federal officials. Plenty of targets here.

Director: But the saying has a sort of David and Goliath feel. The lowly one speaks truth to the great authority. You're hardly a lowly one.

Politician: True, but it's good to cultivate the image that I am.

Director: But I thought you wanted more authority.

Politician: I do. Don't underestimate people's ability to swallow a paradox.

General: People love an underdog. Even if Politician has lots of authority, if he takes on many others with authority, he'll be exactly that.

Director: Is being an underdog associated with being an outsider? People seem to like outsiders, too.

Politician: Yes, they do. The trick is to have lots of insider knowledge while appearing to be an outsider. That wins you votes.

Director: But only with the electorate? I mean, your peers can't like this posturing, can they?

Politician: Most of them try to do it, too. It's simply understood.

General: The funny thing is, I think 'outsiders' tend to speak with more authority, as if they speak with the People's voice, the ultimate source of authority in the land.

Politician: True. That's the point.

Director: Why is it assumed government insider authorities don't speak with the authority of the People's voice?

Politician: The People aren't getting what they want from them. They want healthcare. The insiders haven't delivered. They're not listening to the People's voice.

General: Yes, but the People's voice is divided here. Many don't think the government should be in the business of managing healthcare.

Director: Politician, are you in the business of listening to the People's voice and deciding which part of it speaks with more force?

Politician: And then I follow that part? That suggests I have no principles of my own.

Director: I know that's not true because I've heard you speak truth to the ultimate authority, the People themselves.

General: So have I. And without a principle to support you, you can't speak truth.

Director: But that principle has to align with something the People believe. Otherwise, why would they listen?

Politician: You're right, of course. There has to be something fundamental that we share. Without that, nothing works.

Director: What is this thing you share?

Politician: It can't be put into words.

General: Oh, come on. Of course it can.

Politician: It's a vision.

Director: A vision?

Politician: Of how things should be. Many things go into the vision. That's why I can't spell it all out. But if you listen closely to what I say, and see how people respond, you can tell.

Director: I listened closely to you a few times while you were on television. You were laying the groundwork for healthcare reform. People at work who saw you thought you showed much promise. Why do you think that is?

Politician: Because I tell it like it is, for one. But also, I think people get the sense I have the drive to get it done.

Director: The drive, yes. I think that's true. And the more people respond to this drive, the more drive you have?

Politician: That's true. We feed off each other. It's a vision of each being strong. I help them; they help me.

Director: And you have to reach a sort of critical mass within the House.

Politician: Exactly. And I need a strong core of allies in the Senate.

Director: How strong will they be if you cut their terms down to two years?

Politician: They'll be subject to the same pressures we face in the House. And I'm an expert, a true authority, on playing on that stress.

Director: You're a manipulator.

Politician: You make it sound so bad. I'm an effective agent of the People. And that's what they want.

41

Director: Do you always give the people what they want?

Politician: No. Sometimes I have to teach them what's best.

General: I thought they know their interests.

Politician: Sometimes things get complicated and they can use a little help.

Director: Are they really teachable?

Politician: Judging from the fact that I can sway opinion polls? Yes.

Director: And when they learn what's best, you're on your way.

Politician: Right.

Director: Well, General, it seems like Politician knows what he's doing. Are we missing anything?

General: I don't know. I can't think of anything right now. But something has occurred to me concerning authority. It seems to me there's a difference between being an authority and having authority.

Director: What's the difference?

General: If you are an authority, in the sense of being an expert on something, that's one thing. But it's another thing entirely to have authority given to you. Being, having.

Director: And it's better to be?

General: That's hard for me to say. I'm an authority on a number of things. But I also have authority that was given to me. My point is this. I wonder if Politician needs both types of authority, or if he can go it with one alone. And if he can go it with one alone, I wonder which one it would be.

Politician: The answer to that is easy. I would choose to be an authority. What about you, Director?

Director: If I had to choose? I would be one, as well. But when those who are authorities are given authority, isn't that best?

Politician: It is. But it doesn't always happen. In my case it will.

General: How can you be so sure?

Politician: I'm patiently building the case that I'm an authority who needs to be given authority to get the job done. I see my progress in the polls.

Director: Are the polls authoritative for you?

Politician: They reflect what people think in a moment of time. I'm not a slave to them, but I take them as part of the People's voice.

General: And if the polls show a turn against your legislation?

Politician: They won't.

Director: And you know because you're an expert on this.

Politician: Just so.

Director: Do you ever lean on the polls as authority?

Politician: I make use of the polls. But I wouldn't say I lean on them. Weak people lean on authority.

Director: Does that apply generally or only concerning polls?

Politician: Generally. Authority should never be a crutch. Crutches never serve the strong. They only serve the weak.

Director: And the weak only serve themselves, not others?

Politician: Exactly so. You have to be strong to serve others.

General: The strong can break a leg and need a crutch for a while. You might need one one day. Any of us might.

Politician: True. But some of us come to love our crutch. That's where the trouble begins.

Director: Why love a crutch?

Politician: I honestly don't know. I just see it happen from time to time.

General: When we come to depend on it, we're afraid we can't do without it.

Politician: Maybe so.

Director: Can you do without the polls?

Politician: I believe I can.

Director: How?

Politician. I can take the People's temperature on my own. It's easy enough when you know how to listen.

General: You have to listen to a broad enough base.

Politician: Yes, and you have to have an instinct on who not to listen to, too.

Director: Is it really an instinct or is it something you can learn?

Politician: Oh, I suppose you can learn it if you're made of the right stuff.

General: That just means you bring out the hidden instinct.

Politician: True.

Director: What would hide an instinct?

Politicians. Too many clouds in your sky. You just need some sun in order to see. How's that?

Director: Pretty good. It might be true. The sun comes out and you learn when to stop up your ears.

General: I often stop up my ears and watch what people do.

Politician: Of course. I watch, as well.

Director: Which is more important to you? To watch or to listen?

Politician: Watch first then listen.

General: I agree. And you, Director?

Director: I tend to listen first then watch.

General: Why?

Director: I want to know what people think.

General: You can learn what people think from what they do.

Director: True. But I'm greedy for their words.

Politician: Greedy? Why?

Director: Words are how we think. But there's an important caveat.

Politician: What?

Director: This only applies for interesting people.

General: What makes someone interesting?

Director: What they do.

Politician: Ha! So you do what we do. We all watch first then listen later.

Director: But sometimes I watch a person moving their mouth. Speaking is doing, after all.

Politician: Oh, you're being a sophist now.

General: But let's press this a bit. What happens if we listen but fail to watch?

Politician: We can be fooled. Both intentionally and unintentionally.

Director: How so?

Politician: There are a lot of liars—intentional. But there may be a greater number who fool themselves about themselves. They do one thing, but believe they're doing another. And this 'another' is what they say. Unintentional.

Director: They're clearly not authorities on themselves.

Politician: No, they're not.

Director: But people who are authorities on themselves, they can still lie.

Politician: Of course. That's why we have to watch very closely what they do.

Director: Well, however it is, I still love to hear the words.

Politician: I find the words to be tiresome. Once I know what I need to know, I mostly turn deaf.

Director: Mostly?

Politician: I have to listen enough to know when to nod and smile. But I'm learning nothing new.

Director: That's a very good point. But when I've reached the point where I'm learning nothing new, I politely bring the conversation to a close. That's an advantage I have over you. You're forced to carry on with your electorate, pretending to listen. When I'm done, I'm done.

General: It's the same with me. I can dismiss a subordinate when I'm done.

Director: And when you have to deal with Congress?

General: I nod and smile.

Politician: I don't deny today's hearing was tiresome. But that's the way we get things done.

Director: Or don't.

Politician: True, true. Maybe when I'm Speaker I'll introduce rules of procedure that make the hearings less soul draining.

Director: Hearings are all about what people say.

Politician: In order to determine what they do.

Director: Why not send the committee to see what they do?

Politician: That would be better. But sometimes I think we need a hearing.

Director: When?

Politician: When we give someone a chance to explain.

Director: That sounds more like a trial to me.

Politician: Sometimes that's what it's like.

Director: The committee is the authority?

Politician: Yes, of course.

Director: Is the one who testifies usually an authority?

Politician: Almost always, yes.

Director: Why do you think that is?

Politician: What interest would they be to the committee if they weren't?

Director: Are you looking for an abuse of authority?

Politician: Often times, yes. But sometimes in the course of our work we have good reason to praise successfully borne responsibility.

Director: Your authority blesses the authority of another.

Politician: Well, I don't know about 'blesses'.

Director: Approves of.

Politician: Yes.

Director: When someone with authority to approve approves, what have we got?

Politician: Official sanction. But 'sanction' is a funny word. A sanction can be a penalty for an act. And a sanction can be official approval of an act.

Director: What an odd word it is. I wonder how those opposite meanings came about.

Politician: It's not so hard to see. Authorities have the ability to praise or blame. The sanction is the act of praising or blaming. So there are positive and negative sanctions.

Director: Count on you to clear it all up. Do you sanction our conversation here tonight?

Politician: I give it my full approval, yes.

Director: Why?

Politician: Because I find it amusing.

Director: Do you sanction all amusing things?

Politician: As a general rule, yes. The amusing isn't harmful. It's a pleasant diversion from the more serious things in life.

Director: Oh. I was taking our conversation seriously.

General: As was I.

Politician: You two need to lighten up. You can learn more when you do.

Director: That sounds like good advice.

General: But it's easy advice from a politician.

Politician: Why would you say that?

General: Because you swoop in, deal with an issue, then fly away—while the rest of us are stuck here on the ground.

Politician: Director, are you stuck?

Director: No.

Politician: So, General, you're the only one stuck. What can we do to help?

General: Walk ten miles in my shoes.

Politician: That won't help you.

General: No, but it might make you understand.

Politician: And that's all you want? A little understanding?

General: A little understanding goes a very long way.

42

Director: Is it fair to say that those who have authority should always understand those who conferred their authority?

General: Yes, but not only those who gave the authority. Also those who are subject to the authority.

Director: What about the grounds for the authority?

General: What do you mean?

Director: Isn't some authority by law?

General: Yes.

Director: That's the ground, the grounding. Shouldn't this be understood?

General: Of course.

Politician: What's to understand?

Director: Well, for one, we have to understand that laws are second to the People as the highest authority in the land. But they're very different than the People.

Politician: How so?

Director: Laws are deaf, dumb, and blind.

Politician: Then it's good that the People have the power to change the laws, and the laws don't have the power to change People!

Director: You don't think following the law changes us?

General: Director has a point. Without laws we're savages. Following law ennobles.

Politician: Ennobles? I don't know about that. Civilizes, maybe. But not ennobles.

Director: What would ennoble?

Politician: Going far beyond what the law requires. 'Thou shalt not kill,' becomes, 'Thou shalt help all live.'

Director: So doctors are noble.

Politician: The good ones are, yes.

Director: Aren't the 'good ones' of anything noble?

Politician: You have a point. Goodness and nobility are one.

Director: Because goodness goes beyond. 'Thou shalt not steal,' becomes, 'Thou shalt give to the poor,' or something like that?

Politician: Something like that, sure.

Director: 'Thou shalt not commit adultery,' becomes—

Politician: Oh, that's not a law. And now you're teasing.

General: It's very much a law in the military code of justice.

Director: So what does it become?

General: 'Thou shalt strengthen the bonds between husband and wife.'

Politician: Or wife and wife, or husband and husband.

General: Sure.

Director: And when we're ennobled, we become an authority?

General: Absolutely.

Director: Politician, I take it you agree. But you said goodness and nobility are one. Does that mean when we're good, we become an authority?

Politician: I suppose it does.

Director: So if half the country is good, half the country is an authority?

Politician: It's more like one-tenth the country is good, and so on.

Director: We can't have majority authority?

Politician: Is it possible? Yes. But it's not what we have today.

Director: What would the world be like where the majority was an authority?

Politician: Unrecognizable to us.

Director: In a good way?

Politician: Why do you even ask?

General: He's asking because he's wondering what the majority would work on the minority.

Politician: What might it work?

General: It might make ennoblement a law. And that spells trouble.

Politician: Why?

General: Laws that prohibit certain things are reasonable. But laws that command you to do, positively do certain things—they're no good.

Politician: Why not?

General: Because what does it do to nobility? It makes it required. And if you require nobility, you destroy the essence of the noble—free will, choice.

Director: Again, General has a point.

Politician: He does.

Director: So we should have a naturally occurring nobility that goes beyond the strictures of the law?

General: Yes.

Politician: I think that's how it has to be.

Director: Because the noble is inherently good.

Politician: Maybe we should say the noble is inherently better than the good.

General: The noble are the best. If everyone is the same, there is no best.

Director: It's all for the best.

Politician: Oh, don't be ironic here. You know it's true.

Director: I do know it's all for the sake of the best.

Politician: General, what do you think? Is he putting 'best' in quotation marks?

General: No, I think he's serious. The best go beyond. And they do it by choice. We need to give people the choice. Without choice, nothing truly great blossoms.

Director: So our authorities should leave room for choice.

General: Absolutely.

Director: And if the choices made surprise?

General: We should expect to be surprised. A little surprise is the spice of life.

Politician: I thought variety was the spice of life.

General: Surprise, variety—it's all the same.

Politician: Hardly. Variety you choose. Surprise is chosen for you.

Director: If you as an authority had to choose, would you allow your people variety or give them surprise?

Politician: I would allow them variety, with a little surprise.

Director: Why?

Politician: The variety keeps them interested. The surprise keeps them on their toes.

Director: You don't want your people to be complacent.

Politician: No, I don't. Surprise makes the complacent think twice.

General: I'm happy if my troops think once.

Director: Think, think twice—what's the difference here?

General: If you think, you can know. If you have to think twice, you doubt what you know.

Director: Politician, do you want your people to doubt what they know?

Politician: I want them to doubt what they think they know.

General: But what they think they know includes both what they know and what they really don't know.

Politician: Then they should doubt it all.

General: That will paralyze them. You can't really mean it.

Politician: To the contrary. You can doubt and act quite well. The doubt causes fear, and fear is a spur. Director?

Director: Authorities often use fear as a spur.

Politician: There, you see?

General: What authorities often do isn't necessarily good!

Politician: So how do you spur your troops? With love?

General: With reasons why they should do what they do.

Politician: I'm not sure how you made it to the rank you hold with that kind of philosophy. Who has time to reason in war?

General: Those who would win. And even if they don't win, they win the defeat.

Politician: Win the defeat. That sounds profound. Director, what do you think?

Director: Philosophy often wins the defeat against those who hold authority.

Politician: What does that mean?

Director: If I'm arguing against an authority, the authority might force me to 'lose'. But those present might understand this, and think I should have won. They go away and think this through, and question the authority that 'won'.

Politician: The questioning is the win?

Director: The questioning is the prelude to a win.

General: What's the win?

Director: Striking out on your own.

Politician: Against authority?

Director: With the faults of authority clearly in mind.

General: This is the authority of traveling our own way.

Politician: There's a joy in traveling our own way.

Director: It's not always a joy.

General: What is it?

Director: Sometimes it's... worse.

Politician: Worse? How so 'worse'?

Director: It's simply not always a joy. And when it's not, you have to look it in the eye—and smile.

General: Why do you smile?

Director: Because you know you're an authority here.

General: An authority on worse?

Director: An authority on seeing right through it.

Politician: Who can see right through it?

Director: A philosopher.

Politician: Of course. How?

Director: How does a soldier see through worse?

General: The soldier knows there's something more, something better.

Director: That's what the philosopher knows.

Politician: And the politician?

Director: He or she milks the worse for all it's worth.

43

Politician: So philosophers have more in common with soldiers than politicians?

Director: I don't know that I'd say that. But the things in common are real.

General: What do philosophers have in common with politicians?

Politician: I'll tell you. Both of us believe in the greater good.

General: But the 'greater good' can be used to hide baser things. I've seen if often enough.

Director: What sort of 'baser things', General?

General: Lust for any number of things, including revenge. But mostly? Ambition.

Director: Philosophers never hide ambition.

Politician: Never?

Director: What ambition do philosophers have?

Politician: The fact that we don't know raises serious doubts.

General: Not all of us are driven like you.

Politician: You must be getting old, because you were once driven like this.

General: And maybe now I'm wise. It's good to have ambitions, sure. But it's better to keep them in perspective. All those with authority should 'get old' this way.

Politician: What happens to philosophers who get old?

Director: They die.

Politician: Ha!

Director: But it's true. Philosophy has no desire to live into over-ripe old age.

Politician: Who does?

General: We should say what 'over-ripe' means.

Politician: It's when you've lost your mind. But wait! That counts philosophy out.

Director: How so?

Politician: Philosophy is the pursuit of your own lost mind! Ha!

Director: And once found it's the pursuit of others who've lost their minds.

Politician: Is that what you do? Seek lost souls and help them with their minds?

Director: I can only help if the person is already searching in earnest.

Politician: How can you tell if they're earnest?

Director: They're in pain.

General: I agree. Pain speaks truth.

Politician: But you want to free them of their pain?

Director: That pain, yes. But I'd introduce a new pain. The pain that comes of effort.

Politician: Philosophy's effort.

Director: Yes.

Politician: But what is philosophy's effort?

Director: To get at the truth.

Politician: About the mind?

Director: For one, certainly, yes. But other things, too.

Politician: Why are philosophers special in this? Don't we all make an effort to know?

Director: I'm surprised you even put the question.

Politician: Alright, I was a little hasty. We don't all make an effort to know.

General: Few of us make an effort to know. So is that what philosophy is? The effort to know?

Director: It's a big part of it, but there's more.

Politician: What more?

Director: It would take a long time to explain.

Politician: We're stuck in a blizzard. Explain away.

Director: It has to do with authority. Philosophy questions authority.

Politician: So do non-philosophers.

Director: But philosophy questions because it wants to know.

General: What does it want to know?

Director: If authority can be good.

Politician: The authority or the person with it?

Director: Both. But especially the person with it.

Politician: Well, just ask General or me. We both seem 'good', don't we?

Director: Sure, but I've never seen you when you exercise your authority. You two are relaxed here tonight. It's a sort of holiday from your responsibilities. Philosophy wants to know what you are when you're fully engaged.

Politician: Then come to the capital more often and see. You're formally invited.

General: Why don't you come to Command on a contractor's pass? I could use some consulting on operations.

Politician: That's better. Come and consult for me, as well.

Director: Thank you both. I'll talk with my boss and see what we can do.

Politician: You should go out on your own. No boss. With references like General and me, you'll be on your way.

Director: But philosophy comes before consulting. Can you go along with that?

Politician: Sure.

Director: Even if philosophy asks awkward questions?

Politician: Why would they be awkward?

Director: They might be embarrassing.

General: Director, don't be afraid to embarrass yourself with what you don't know.

Director: Thank you, General. I make a point not to. But I was thinking my questions might be embarrassing to Politician.

Politician: How could you possibly embarrass me?

Director: Your staff would be around when I ask.

Politician: Oh, but that's not the time for philosophy. When you consult, you have to stick to the business at hand. You and I can talk philosophy later.

General: You can ask me philosophical questions any time, Director. My staff knows me well. There will be no embarrassment here. They and I would hope to learn something from you.

Politician: Well, General, I can't let you show me up. So, Director, you can ask your questions whenever you will. I'll be on my best behavior. I promise.

Director: But that's the thing. I want to see your typical behavior, so I can judge whether authority is good for you.

Politician: You really can't tell from talking to me now?

Director: I really can't.

General: He wants to see the dark side of the moon. Behind the scenes. A typical day. We'll get you cleared so you can see that with me.

Politician: I just don't see the point. If authority were bad for me, you'd see it in me now.

Director: Things might be fine for a while. But over time? That's what I want to judge.

Politician: Well, I'll judge you right back. Is philosophy good for you, over time? I'll follow you around to see.

Director: You haven't got the time.

Politician: But if I had the time?

Director: We probably wouldn't be having this conversation.

General: That's a good point.

Politician: Yes, but how did we get off on this tangent, anyway? And why are we even talking about authority?

Director: In order to while away the night.

General: Yes. This is a fine way to spend it. I haven't looked at any of my messages! Ha, ha! There will be hell to pay! But it's worth it.

Director: Is that wise?

General: Oh, if there's an emergency they have ways of letting me know. I'm still on the leash. But it's nice to get away from the noise.

44

Politician: Is that what philosophy is? Entertainment? A distraction from more serious things?

Director: Philosophy wants you to think. Depending how you're disposed toward thought, the answer will differ.

Politician: How are you disposed toward thought?

Director: Favorably.

General: Ha, ha. So am I. And you, Politician?

Politician: I make the electorate think.

Director: How do you manage that?

Politician: I take what they say they want and then tell them what it entails. That makes them think.

Director: And if it entails you doing all the work and them watching from the stands? There's not much thought there, I'd think.

General: I agree. I don't see how you can make the voters think. They'll think what they think.

Politician: Yes, but I can give them the facts. The facts make people think.

General: Or the facts scare them away.

Director: I think you do something else, Politician. I think you make people believe.

Politician: That's true. I do, and I'm very good at it. We need belief. It's in very short supply.

Director: I don't believe you on that. But you do seem to have an ability to make people in general believe. I'd say you're an authority on that.

General: I would, too.

Politician: Someone has to lead, and that someone leads through belief. That's why I want to speak as Speaker of the House.

Director: You need a grand enough platform to get the message out.

Politician: Yes, though I think you're teasing me now.

Director: No, I really think your project must involve the proper platform.

General: When you have the platform, what would you have them believe?

Politician: First, in themselves. They need to know they're the greatest People there ever was. That helps to unify them.

Director: Why do you need them unified?

Politician: So they can all get behind the legislation and put pressure on their Congresspeople. That makes my job so much easier.

General: But not all of them will want the legislation.

Politician: They need to understand that the legislation will make us even greater.

Director: Greater than greatest is pretty good. Hard to argue with that.

Politician: And they will believe it—because it's true.

Director: What's the hallmark of greatness?

Politician: Doing great things.

Director: Like winning the war?

Politician: Of course. And passing watershed legislation.

Director: Things will be different on the other side of this legislation, just as they were different after the war.

Politician: They certainly will.

Director: And you will be famous for this for decades to come.

Politician: Centuries.

Director: That may be. So long as it doesn't get repealed after you're gone.

Politician: Yes, that is a worry.

General: How can you prevent it?

Politician: It has to work well enough that it becomes a part of the fabric of the Nation.

Director: There's no belief in that. It works or it doesn't.

Politician: True. It's getting there that needs belief.

General: I think in all things it's the getting there that needs belief.

Director: You two can become authorities on getting there.

General: I wouldn't mind that.

Politician: Neither would I. We just have to make sure 'there' lives up to people's belief.

General: Very true. But what about you, Director? Why can't you become an authority on getting there? Can't philosophy help us get to peace of mind?

Politician: What peace of mind is there if you're constantly thinking?

General: There can be peace in thought. Director?

Director: Thinking is thinking. What makes for peace, or not, is external to thought.

Politician: You don't really believe that.

Director: You're right. I don't believe—I know.

Politician: Ha! Now we see your true colors.

Director: What color is truth?

General: Oh, he's teasing you, Politician. But I'd like to hear more about the things external to thought.

Director: It's quite simple, actually. Let's say you're subject to an authority that believes A and seeks to make others believe in A. Your whole society is permeated with A. When you think critically of A, aren't you less likely to be at peace than you would if you thought about B, a B that no one is trying to enforce and no one really believes?

Politician: Yes, but this is only for critical thought.

Director: Is there another kind?

General: Hold on a minute. All thought is a sort of tearing down?

Director: There's criticism, and then there's constructive criticism.

General: Ah, of course. It's hard to criticize what everyone believes, or claims to believe. And when you think that way, it might not bring you peace of mind. In fact, it might bring inner turmoil.

Director: Yes, exactly my point. But if A is a thing of the past, it's no trouble at all.

Politician: But every age has its A. Are you saying philosophers that think about A are in inner turmoil all the time?

Director: You can get to a point where you're simply puzzled by A. But this state can be hard to achieve. And now it's clear I shouldn't have said what makes for peace is simply external to thought. There's an internal component, too.

General: What steps can someone take to reach the puzzled stage?

Director: You have to get comfortable with doubt.

Politician: That's it?

Director: That's no small thing.

Politician: But what do you doubt? Everything?

Director: At times it seems that way. That's when you test your mettle.

General: But you get out of this stage and doubt only... the dubious?

Director: Yes.

Politician: Ha, ha. But everything seems dubious to you.

Director: Not so. Some things are very sure. Many things, in fact.

Politician: What's something you doubt?

Director: Authority. But I do more than doubt. I question.

General: We've all been questioning each other tonight. And that's as it should be.

Politician: Is that all you do, Director? Question?

Director: It seems to me I could do less.

General: Questioning is hard, Politician—and you know it.

Politician: Oh? Have we been having a hard time tonight?

Director: Questioning is best among friends. I like to think we're friends.

General: We are. And I agree. But tell us why it's best among friends. I'd like to hear you say.

Director: Friends are more open to one another. Their questions can go deeper.

Politician: It's as simple as that?

Director: In my experience? Yes.

General: It only makes sense.

Politician: Yes, but friendly conversation lacks that certain spark of controversy you can have with others.

General: But then people are bent on attacking and defending, not on truth. I don't know about you, but friends for me have a spark of their own.

Politician: Don't you believe in the adversarial process in our courts? It's the best way to get at the truth.

General: If you take your truth from the courts, I don't know what to tell you. They get it wrong half the time.

Director: Maybe I've got it wrong.

Politician: How so?

Director: Some friends aren't open to one another. They fit themselves into superficial roles when they interact. There's nothing deep going on here.

General: Yes, that happens all the time. But, Director—they're not really friends. True friends interact fully. Not all the time, of course; but on occasion, on important occasions—when there's a need.

Politician: What if there's never a need?

General: What do you mean?

Politician: Some people go through life with hardly a need to go deep. They're authorities on the shallow.

Director: Are there authorities on the deep?

Politician: Yes, of course. They thrive on getting down into the muck.

Director: There's not always muck in the depths. Some people's depths are clean.

Politician: And you're an authority on this 'clean'?

Director: I am.

Politician: What's in the depths that's clean?

Director: Thoughts, thoughts that have been made clean through articulation.

Politician: What does that mean?

Director: You spell it all out—sometimes to yourself, sometimes to others. Each time you spell it out, you clear up all the muck.

General: It's like regular house cleaning.

Director: Exactly. Some people think they can think their way to a conclusion, and then that's it. But it takes regular thinking to keep things clean.

Politician: So what makes you an authority? You keep yourself clean?

Director: Yes, I try to keep myself clean. I allow others to inspect; and I, in turn, inspect others. I've done this enough that I know what I'm looking for.

General: What are you looking for?

Director: Contradictions, hopes disguised as facts, and so on.

Politician: Emotions disguised as truths?

Director: Emotions are truths of their own. They're facts to be considered. But when emotions color thought, distort thought—that's where I step in.

General: What do you do?

Director: I simply walk them through the thought in the naked light.

Politician: The naked light of reason.

Director: Yes.

Politician: So you're claiming to be an authority on reason?

Director: On a particular use of reason.

General: Its use for hygiene.

Politician: What are you, Director, some sort of physician?

Director: In a sense. But I can't help just anyone.

Politician: Of course not. You can only help the easy cases.

Director: Not all of the cases I work with are easy.

Politician: Am I one of your cases?

Director: Let me say who I can help, then you tell me. I said I'm looking for contradictions and things disguised. If nearly everything in a person is contradictory and disguised, there's not much I can do. But if things are mostly clear, I can help with the rest.

Politician: Like I said—you take the easy cases.

Director: People who are mostly clear take pride in the fact. They recognize that not everyone is so. So when I come along and say, 'Look, you're not as clear as you think,' they sometimes have bad reactions.

General: They lash out at you.

Director: They sometimes do.

Politician: Why lash out if they're mostly clear?

Director: Because they realize that the part that isn't clear is a sort of keystone to their personality.

General: I think I know what you mean. This all has to be handled with great care—by both parties.

Director: Yes, that's true.

General: You never really take an easy case, do you?

Director: Sure I do. Sometimes I notice a little thing and make a comment in passing. The person smiles and makes the change. Easy.

Politician: Why do you take on the harder cases?

Director: It's my calling in life. And it helps me with myself, keeping myself clean.

Politician: How?

Director: The problems I see in others help me avoid them, or correct them, in myself.

General: It's easier to see problems in others than it is in ourselves.

Director: That's why conversations with friends are so important. They help us see ourselves. Friends should find ways to shine light on each other so both can see.

General: So it's not one authority over the other. It's each as an authority to the other.

Director: And that's a beautiful thing.

45

General: Politician, can you imagine if all of the People were authorities to each other—you included—and you to them?

Politician: Honestly? I can't. At most I can see maybe ten percent like this—and that after lots and lots of work. And how will the other ninety percent feel about them, us?

General: Who cares?

Politician: I care. The People have to be united. This will divide.

Director: Do you think the ninety will resent the ten?

Politician: Of course they will, in many and various ways, for many and various things.

Director: Can you give an example?

Politician: Oh, just use your imagination. In the ninety, some will be authorities over others. They'll see the equality—the authority-to—practiced by the ten and feel it as a threat. They'll poison the people of the ninety against them.

General: I think he has a point. But we can't let that stop us. A better way is a better way, no matter if some don't like it. I want to be an authority-to, not an authority-over.

Politician: Even to your troops?

General: Who knows? Maybe this would work there, too. Each and every soldier is more of an authority than I on something. I need to recognize that, just as they need to recognize my authority to command. I want to look them in the eye, not look down on them.

Politician: I, too, would rather look eye-to-eye than down.

General: So take as much authority-to as you can get, and try for more whenever you can.

Politician: That's what I'll do—provided too many others don't resent my authority-to.

General: Oh, stop your worries. How many people really have a vested interest in authority-over?

Politician: Those who are over, and a surprising number of those who are under.

Director: Why those who are under?

Politician: They're used to getting their answers from on high. Try changing that and see what you get.

General: You're talking about dependencies.

Politician: Yes, I am.

Director: What's the reaction if you approach an 'under' as an authority-to?

Politician: They don't know how to act. They think you're rude. They see you as doing something wrong. They might even consider you to be immoral.

General: Immoral? Why?

Politician: Authorities-over almost always set the moral tone. This tone is the musical key for many unders' lives. Along we come singing a different tune in a very different key. How do you think they'll react?

General: Some will like our tune.

Politician: And some will run away, taking others with them as they flee.

Director: So you want to sing an over-tune, to keep them all in line?

Politician: No, I just don't want to drive them away in droves.

Director: Hmm. Maybe there's a neutral tune.

Politician: A tune without authority?

General: Maybe in politics that's the best you can do.

Politician: And what about your tune? You don't think authority-to will meet resistance where you work?

General: The ones who resist don't deserve to be there. It's easy enough to block promotions, give undesirable assignments, and so on. I can weed them out over time.

Politician: I don't have that luxury. I have to approach this like a bull fighter would.

Director: The People are a bull?

Politician: Oh, not the People. The authority-over crowd.

Director: I would cheer you as you fight. But tell us. Is there ever a time when authority-over is good?

Politician: If people aren't capable of authority-to, for whatever reason, and the situation calls for authority, authority-over might be the only choice.

Director: What's an example?

Politician: Children.

General: But children respond better to authority-to. They know you have the power of command with them, but love knowing they can be authorities to you with things they themselves command.

Politician: Wait until they become teenagers.

General: Authority-to is still the way.

Director: General, is there ever a time when authority-over is the way?

General: I don't think so.

Director: And yet there are those who employ it. Why?

General: Maybe they're insecure. Authority-to takes a good deal of confidence on both sides.

Politician: There's something to that. But the problem is the insecure still need to be led. They don't respond well to authority-to. They need authority-over.

General: Maybe in a crisis, when there's nothing else to be done. But authority-to should be the goal.

Director: Isn't there always some crisis or other?

Politician: Whether manufactured or real, there almost always is.

Director: Would you ever manufacture a crisis?

Politician: If I would, why would I tell you? Besides, healthcare already is a crisis.

General: Not for all.

Politician: If it's a crisis for many, it's a crisis for all. No?

General: You have a point.

Director: Politician, is that what you like to focus on? Crises?

Politician: Where else would I focus?

Director: I understand the politics. But you, do you like them?

Politician: Crises? I do.

Director: That makes you unusual. Most people dread crises. Why do you think you like them?

Politician: They allow me to show what I'm made of.

Director: And if you're made of the right stuff, people want to give you the authority to deal with the crises, because they don't want to deal with them themselves.

Politician: 'They don't want to' is generous. Mostly they can't. I fill the void.

Director: The void in your self?

Politician: The void in the situation. But you may have a point. I haven't looked at it that way before. Filling a void to fill a void. Somehow that makes sense.

General: We all have voids to fill. I fill mine with family and work.

Director: Is what you're thinking of a void, or is it love?

Politician: Longing for love is a void.

General: I love my family, but I wouldn't say I long for them. And I certainly don't long for my work.

Politician: Maybe you do.

General: What do you mean?

Politician: If you're away from work for long, do you miss it?

General: I do.

Politician: How badly do you miss it?

General: Badly enough that I want it back.

Politician: Suppose you were away for a month.

General: I couldn't be away for a month.

Politician: Would it kill you?

General: Figuratively speaking, yes.

Politician: Then I would say you long for work.

General: I must admit you have a point. Director, what do you long for?

Director: More philosophy.

Politician: What does that mean?

Director: More conversations like this.

Politician: That's really all you want?

Director: Well, it's what I want most.

Politician: I'll never understand that.

General: You don't like our conversation?

Politician: Oh, sure I do. It's pleasant, stimulating, even a little fun. But is that the best I know in life? Hardly.

Director: You're looking for the big win.

Politician: Yes, and everything goes to that.

Director: I'm looking for conversation, and everything goes to that.

Politician: Suit yourself, but I don't see the point.

General: Director, you really don't have a higher aim?

Director: My aim is to introduce philosophy where there is none. Isn't that a higher aim?

General: You're a teacher.

Director: And a student. Philosophy goes both ways.

46

General: And the authority in philosophy is always authority-to?

Director: When there's authority, that's what it is.

Politician: Are you saying there are times when there is no authority?

Director: Certainly. Neither of us might know what we're talking about.

Politician: So what do you do, grope around in the dark?

Director: We start by trying to light candles.

Politician: What are the candles?

Director: Little things we know. If we keep on building on them, soon we might have enough light to make out bigger things.

Politician: And when you make them out, you light them aflame?

Director: The metaphor only goes so far, but yes.

Politician: A world on fire. That's philosophy?

Director: I'd rather you said it's a world of light.

Politician: What's the darkness? Ignorance?

Director: Ignorance certainly isn't the light. But I think we should drop the candle metaphor now.

Politician: Why?

Director: Because there's literal darkness inside of us. And we light our insides not with candles, but words.

Politician: Words are strange things.

General: How so?

Politician: If we were all alone, we'd never develop words. Words exist to communicate with others. They're shaped by both ourselves and others as we go back and forth in conversation. Each word is a sort of little agreement—a contract, if you will. We bind ourselves to the meaning.

General: That's interesting, but I don't see the point.

Politician: When we look inside ourselves with words, we're using tools in large part designed by others.

General: I see what you mean. Director?

Director: That's why we have to make the words our own.

General: How do we do that?

Director: We become an authority with them.

Politician: But what does that mean? You bend the meaning of the words to your will?

Director: Not quite. I take the meaning from others. I take it on trust.

Politician: See how far that gets you. What then?

Director: Then I hold fast. I don't let the meaning slip away.

General: And if it slips away? Not because you let go, but because the other slips away?

Director: I consider that a breach of trust.

Politician: I'd consider it a breach of implied contract. You should seek restitution! Ha, ha.

General: So what do you do, Director?

Director: I seek to clear things up. Here I am with this meaning divorced from its source.

General: So how do you make things clear?

Director: I have to start all over again, word by word. I have to make sure the words and I have good agreement each step along the way.

Politician: You and your words. So where are you stepping to?

Director: We're stepping toward the light.

General: And when you arrive there your authority-with is in place?

Politician: What are we even talking about? You're trying to have authority-with with words?

Director: Yes, so I can speak intelligibly with others. If both parties don't have authority-with with words, clear communication is impossible.

General: People think it's simple to have good agreement on words. But I'm with you—it's surprisingly hard to achieve!

Politician: What makes it hard?

Director: I'm not sure, exactly. But people don't always like to be held to their words. 'Oh, it's just a figure of speech.' 'Oh, I didn't mean that literally.' 'Oh, you know what I mean.' They say things like that.

Politician: I've noticed. But then chasing all these things down makes you the most tiresome man in the room!

Director: I only chase them down with people of interest.

Politician: What makes a person 'of interest'?

Director: They're not satisfied with their use of words.

Politician: And you would help them break their words down and build them back up.

Director: Yes, I would. And I break mine down in the process, too.

Politician: Why bother if you already have authority with your words?

Director: Think of it like a rifle. You take it apart and clean it so you know it will work. That's what I do with my words on a regular basis. I want to know they'll work.

Politician: But you won't know until you try them out with others.

Director: True. And if they don't, I suspect my words weren't clean and I break them down again.

Politician: And if they work?

Director: It's still a good habit to give them a cleaning. After all, my interlocutor and I might have been fooled into thinking they worked. Subsequent review might show it was otherwise.

General: You're very thorough in what you do.

Director: It's a labor of love.

Politician: You love the authority that comes from good words?

Director: I love the effect that comes from good words.

General: Light.

Director: Light, yes; but also appropriate contrast and shade.

General: Like a good drawing.

Director: Exactly. Words should depict, describe. And I like them best when they describe difficult things.

General: Sometimes the simple is the most difficult.

Director: Perfectly so. And what's simpler than authority? We all know it when we see it. Don't we?

General: In both its good and bad forms, yes.

Director: We know the good and the bad right away?

General: Well, maybe not always right away. It takes some experience to know.

Director: When we know, it's important to describe authority for what it is. Yes?

General: Yes, it's very important. Everyone needs to be clear.

Director: If someone believes in a false authority, what do we do?

General: Tell them the truth. The sooner the better.

Politician: You'll just scare them off. You need to be gentle.

Director: What would you say?

Politician: I'd ask them seemingly innocuous questions leading to my point.

General: You sound like a philosopher.

Politician: How would you know what a philosopher sounds like?

General: I read some philosophy at the Academy. And you?

Politician: I read a little in college.

Director: Did you enjoy it?

Politician: I thought it was funny.

General: Funny?

Politician: A lot of fuss over nothing.

General: You don't think ideas are important?

Politician: Yes, but they're best dealt with in public debate.

Director: I couldn't agree with you less.

Politician: You don't believe in public debate?

Director: I don't. Private debate is more effective.

Politician: You say that because philosophy shuns the light.

Director: The limelight? Some philosophers thrive in it. I've never been in it so I wouldn't know to shun it or not.

General: Why private, Director?

Director: There's usually less pressure. And when there's less pressure people tend to be more open.

General: Depending on who's in the room.

Director: Yes, of course. But philosophers are sometimes good at getting people to relax, to let down their guard.

Politician: How do they do that?

Director: They show they're not trying to win.

General: You can't say that about most public debate.

Politician: No, that's true.

Director: And I wouldn't even call it private debate. I'd call it conversation, dialogue. Something like that. Something where everyone can win.

General: Even so, not everyone will be open to this sort of conversation.

Director: That's why we're highly selective in what we say to whom.

General: You don't say the same thing to everyone?

Director: Does a doctor give everyone the same advice?

Politician: See? It's a sham conversation.

Director: Is a doctor-patient conversation a sham?

Politician: Of course not. But I'd hardly call it a dialogue. If it were a true dialogue the patient could give the doctor advice.

General: He has a point, Director.

Director: And that's the limit of the medical metaphor. Because those I speak with certainly do, at times, give me very good advice. But it's really all a sort of crime.

Politician: Ha! What?

Director: We're like burglars trying to crack the lock on a safe.

General: What's inside the safe?

Director: The person's heart.

Politician: So what does that make you, Director? An authority on the human heart?

Director: That's not for me to say. But I know people who think that's true.

Politician: Do you encourage them in that belief?

Director: No, the opposite, in fact.

Politician: Because you don't want authority? You don't want the responsibility?

Director: No one can be responsible for someone else's heart.

Politician: Not even in love?

Director: Lovers care for each other's heart. But we can only be responsible for our own.

Politician: Then why do we speak of breaking someone's heart? Surely we're responsible for that.

Director: No, we're not.

General: Director, I've known some rogues who have broken many hearts. They are, no doubt, responsible.

Politician: They're authorities on broken hearts. Ha, ha.

Director: How do you break someone's heart? How does it happen?

General: They're in love with you, but you're not in love with them. And you take advantage of the situation.

Director: Are you doing what they want?

General: Well, yes, in a sense.

Politician: No you're not. What they really want is for you to be in love with them.

Director: And a rogue pretends to be in love.

Politician: Exactly. So what are you going to say, Director? We're all responsible to know this 'love' for what it is?

General: Of course not. The rogues take advantage of those with little experience in love. How can these poor people be responsible?

Director: Would you say the rogues are authorities on love?

General: No. They're authorities on manipulation.

Director: What's their responsibility?

General: They should manipulate people to see the truth of the situation and gently help them out of love.

Director: And if that makes them fall even more deeply in love?

General: Then the rogues need to be cruel to be kind—and break things off.

Director: And then the one with the broken heart has the responsibility to put it back together again. Or should they just wallow?

General: No, you're right. We all have some responsibility for our hearts. And when we put them back together, we're that much closer to being authorities on ourselves.

Politician: Hearts heal stronger than they were before they broke.

General: Sometimes that's true.

Director: Have you ever had a broken heart?

General: Yes, when I was in high school. I fell very hard, was strung along, then learned the truth that she never loved me. It broke my heart.

Director: Did the break happen all at once?

General: No, it took a tortured several years to accept the fact that she didn't love me.

Politician: Better to break at once.

General: I don't know. I learned a lot during those several years. I healed as I broke, if that makes sense.

Director: It does. But what did you learn?

General: How to guard my heart.

Director: You closed yourself off?

General: For a time.

Politician: When did you open again? With your wife?

General: Oh, Politician, that's such a private thing. I'd rather not get into details. The point is that I became an authority on my heart.

Politician: Okay. But does anyone have authority-over with your heart?

General: No one—though my wife has authority-to with my heart, as I have authority-to with hers.

Politician: You're authorities on each other's heart, and bear the responsibility that comes of it.

General: That's what happens when you know each other well.

Politician: I know some people well who aren't my wife. Do I have responsibility for them?

General: With knowledge comes responsibility.

Politician: And with responsibility borne well comes authority? Are we still saying that?

General: Yes.

Politician: So knowledge can make you an authority if you bear your responsibility well.

General: Certainly.

Politician: But what responsibility are we talking about? I know a lot about cars. That makes me an authority. There's no responsibility here.

General: You have the responsibility not to mislead.

Politician: Everyone has the responsibility not to mislead. So as I said, there's no responsibility, outside the normal responsibilities, here.

Director: Is there ever a time when 'normal' responsibilities don't apply?

Politician: Sure. During war. We want to mislead the enemy.

Director: General?

General: That's true.

Director: So are we saying something like this? We're only responsible to our own.

General: Well, there are foreigners and strangers who might come here and be friendly to us even though they're not 'our own'. Unless they prove to be enemies, we're responsible not to mislead them.

Director: It's a sort of bond of hospitality?

General: Yes, we can put it that way. I would expect the same if visiting them.

Director: If you bear your responsibility of being a host well, does that make you an authority on hospitality?

General: That sounds a little strange, but I suppose it's true.

Director: Why does it sound strange?

General: Some things we don't think of that way.

Director: Should we?

General: I don't think it would do any harm.

Director: But would it do any good?

Politician: I don't think it would. It seems pointless.

Director: Can we say that any authority that seems pointless isn't worth our time?

Politician: Yes, of course.

Director: And if others take up pointless authority, that's not worth our time either?

General: Definitely not.

Politician: Not worth a minute, no.

Director: But what if someone insists? 'I'm the authority here; you must heed.'

Politician: I would laugh in their face and walk away.

Director: And if they have legal authority?

Politician: That's a bird of a different feather.

Director: You mean you might laugh but you can't walk away?

Politician: Even laughter here spells trouble.

Director: So what do we do?

Politician: Change the law and take the authority away.

Director: Is it a quick thing to change the law?

Politician: Of course not.

Director: So we have to suffer this pointless authority for a while.

Politician: I'm afraid so.

Director: One bit of pointlessness might not be much. But what if there are a number of these authorities?

Politician: It's obviously a problem, one that might take more priority because of the effect.

Director: What is the effect?

Politician: Oppression.

General: I agree.

Director: What's the nature of the oppression?

Politician: The amount of authority we're subject to should be limited to the necessary.

Director: And if it isn't?

Politician: Our freedom is diminished.

Director: Authority diminishes freedom?

Politician: Pointless authority does.

Director: Ah, I see. But why?

Politician: Because it gets in the way.

Director: Let me see if I understand. Pointlessness diminishes, while pointedness enhances?

General: That's an excellent point. Authority with a point enhances our freedom. It protects our freedom. It makes our freedom real.

Politician: Oh, you take it too far. Freedom needs authority to help protect it, agreed. But that's as far as it goes. Your authority as a general, and mine as a legislator—that's about as much authority as we need.

Director: Do you mean that literally? Law and defense? That's it?

Politician: Why not? I'm sure people would cry out that we need someone to execute the laws and oversee the defense. But I don't see why the legislature can't create bodies for both.

General: But, ultimately, one person needs to decide.

Politician: Why? Why not a body of three, or whatever?

General: But they would answer to the legislature.

Politician: After their term. Until then, I'd give them free rein. Unless, of course, they go too far out of line.

Director: They might abuse their authority.

Politician: Yes. We'd have provisions for this.

General: You just want to do away with the President as a rival.

Politician: And the Court, too. The legislature is all. What do you think?

General: I think we need our checks and balances.

Politician: Times are changing quickly. We need to adapt. The threat of Presidential veto slows us down. And the Court? That's a wildcard we don't need. We need to be sure about our laws, not wonder if they'll hold up.

Director: But is the legislature really the only authority we need?

Politician: You're like the slow one in school. Yes, that's all we need.

Director: Literally?

Politician: Why are you stuck on this? Literally, yes.

Director: No authority of parents to children?

Politician: What? Of course not that! I'm talking about government.

Director: Oh. I thought you might be talking about everything.

General: The way he talks, I can't blame you.

Politician: You two are nuts. Private authority stays intact. Public authority concentrates in Congress.

Director: But you do know you can't change public authority without changing private authority, and the other way round—don't you?

Politician: Tell me how this would be.

Director: Private authority's effect on public authority is simple. Changes in the private put pressure on the public, especially when the leaders are elected.

Politician: Of course.

Director: But changes in the public are a little harder to trace in their effect. Certain people look up to the public and model their behavior there. This changes their private interactions, and over time the effect spreads and has some power. Does that make sense?

Politician: It makes sense. So you're saying my changes would have more effect than I thought. And I say that's good!

General: It would be easier for me to consider this rationally if I didn't think it was all a scheme to make you the most powerful man in the world. Why not just run for President?

Politician: Congress has the power of the purse. I don't want to be a cash starved President. And I don't just think this for my sake. No leader should have to go begging for money.

Director: But you'd have to beg for funds in Congress, no?

Politician: Beg? Not with my authority.

General: Look at him smile. Apparently, authority is good for cash.

Politician: So it is. Director, what do you think?

Director: You'd dismantle the structure of our government in order to play to your strength. What am I supposed to think?

Politician: So you agree it can be done?

Director: Sure, it can be done. But what comes after you're gone? Or will you put it all back together again before you go?

Politician: No, I won't put it back the way it was. What will come? Ineffective leadership, probably.

Director: Do you feel good about that?

Politician: I'll take someone under my wing and train them in my ways. A successor.

General: That rarely works.

Director: Why?

General: It's one thing to watch the game from inside and really know it; it's another thing to play.

47

Director: You need to have the authority yourself.

General: Yes, that's the only way.

Politician: But I don't have that authority yet, and neither of you are saying I won't do well. Why?

General: We believe in you.

Politician: Director?

Director: I believe you have great potential. That's why I'm not saying you won't do well.

Politician: So why can't I pick someone with great potential to take under my wing?

Director: They wouldn't have it. Would you?

Politician: Honestly? No. I don't want to be under a wing. I want to take to my wings.

General: That's all the difference here. But I think you need a good rival, one who comes at you with everything they've got.

Politician: Rivalry sharpens the edge. And you can believe I'd use all my authority against them.

Director: As you should.

Politician: I would try to break them.

Director: Again, as you should. After all, they will try to do that to you.

General: Look at Politician. He's excited! That tells me he's going where he should.

Politician: We should all go where we're excited.

Director: Regardless of cost?

Politician: The only real cost in life is if we forego excitement for something else.

Director: What 'something else'?

Politician: Fears, mostly. But we hide this truth from ourselves and come up with words like duty, responsibility, obligation, and so on—words that keep us in check.

General: Misused words.

Politician: Precisely.

Director: So it's not that you don't believe in responsibility.

Politician: Right. I don't believe in 'responsibility'. I don't believe in something that drowns out life.

Director: General?

General: True responsibility adds something to life.

Director: I think there's little doubt someone like you has true responsibility.

General: Yes, and I'm lucky. For the most part, my responsibilities lead to excitement. And I know what Politician means. Some of us never leave the farm. Not because the farm excites us. But because we're afraid to go.

Politician: Director, you should preach a philosophy of excitement. You'd be doing real good.

Director: Yes, but there are problems here. Criminals are probably excited when they commit their crimes. Are they where they should be?

Politician: Well, of course there are exceptions. People have to follow the law. And I would like to make laws that make things more exciting.

Director: Another problem is that excitement often involves danger. Exciting laws may jeopardize the country. Is that a price you'd pay?

Politician: No risk, no reward. There are people who'd vote for that.

Director: I'm sure there are. I think desperate people would, among others.

General: Who are the others?

Director: People who don't understand the risk. And those with contingency plans.

General: Parachutes, you mean.

Politician: Don't worry about that. I'll make sure we're all in it together.

Director: Even those who don't vote for you and your plan?

Politician: We're all bought into the system. Sometimes you win; sometimes you lose.

Director: What if we're not all bought in?

Politician: Then the risks are greater.

General: Then the government needs contingency plans. And I don't mean parachutes.

Director: How did our conversation about authority end up here?

Politician: Ultimately, the question of authority is about who rules.

General: The People rule here. The People have the ultimate authority. They can change the law of the land. And for that the People must unite. A divided People can't change fundamental law.

Politician: Assuming they play by the rules for change.

General: If they don't, all bets are off.

Director: I'm not sure what that means. So, Politician, it's up to you to ensure we all follow the rules.

Politician: I will. I have an interest in this—my job.

Director: The stability of the country comes down to your wanting to have your job. I feel safe.

Politician: Ha, ha! And you should! You know I'll do it well.

Director: General, what do you think? Or are you full of gloom and doom?

General: No, I'm not. I worry, that's all. But I do have confidence in Politician. I want to see him succeed. I think the country will be better off with him in a leadership role. But there's nothing I can do to help. That I regret.

Politician: Oh, it's good you play no role in politics. I don't like to think what it would be like if you did!

Director: General, what would happen if you did?

General: If I had political authority? Legitimate authority? Today? I'd set some things straight.

Politician: And that's the problem. If you try to straighten the branch of a tree all at once, it breaks. It takes patience and time. I have patience. And if I keep winning, I'll have time.

Director: Funny, I didn't think of you as having much patience as we talked of your plans.

Politician: Just because the plans are grand doesn't mean I'm not aware of what they'll take.

Director: That makes sense, I think. General, does that make sense?

General: Sense enough.

Director: Yes, but now I'm really not sure. Politician, you know exactly what your plans will take?

Politician: Let's put it this way. I have a pretty good idea. And my idea will gain in focus with every step I take.

General: That's all we can expect.

Director: Yes, I think that's true. And I'm pleased to hear he wants to follow the process.

Politician: Of course I want to follow the process. What else would I do? Arrange a coup? Ha, ha!

General: That happens in other countries. It doesn't happen here. Our forces are loyal.

Director: To whom?

General: To what. The Constitution.

Director: And if the People change the Constitution?

General: We'd be loyal to that. It's been amended plenty of times. And likely will be again.

Director: Military force accepts the authority of the written word. That strikes me as remarkable.

Politician: Can you see now why I want to be a legislator and not an executive? I want to make law, law respected by force.

Director: What would it take for your people, General, not to respect a law? I'm sorry for putting you on the spot.

General: Not at all. We asked questions like this in a leadership course I attended. The only possible law we wouldn't respect is one that subverts the law.

Director: Law subverting law? I don't understand. Can you give an example?

General: Suppose the People amend the Constitution to take the ultimate authority away from the People.

Director: Why would they do that?

General: Who knows? But it's possible.

Politician: It would have to be under an emergency situation.

General: Yes, probably. But what do you think? Should we respect this legal Amendment?

Politician: You'd have to. It would be the law of the land.

Director: I'm not good with hypotheticals like this. Nor am I good with law. But if you don't want trouble, General, I'd say you should respect the law. What did you say in class?

General: I said we must respect the law.

Director: Why?

General: Because we believe in the rule of law.

Director: Why do we believe in the rule of law?

General: Because the rule of men proved so terrible in so many ways.

Politician: Humanity has come a long way.

Director: If it has, is it time to revisit our faith?

Politician: In the law? Why would we do that? But let's suppose we didn't believe in the rule of law. What then?

General: Force would have no check.

Politician: No, General, there would be a check—the authority of men like you.

General: That's a very dangerous game. While I suppose I should thank you for the compliment, I must point out that not everyone is even-tempered and cautious like me.

Director: Is that really all we'd have? The personal authority of women and men?

General: What else would we have? I don't like this turn we've taken.

Politician: Oh, we're just talking, friend.

General: Personal authority is... is... weak! The authority of law is strong.

Director: Not everywhere.

Politician: That's absolutely true.

General: Yes, it's true. And I've been to those places. And let me tell you—you don't want to live there.

Director: Hmm. It occurs to me that we have a strange institution concerning the authority of law. The Supreme Court. It says when laws aren't to be treated as laws.

General: Because they're unconstitutional.

Director: Yes. But the personal authority of the Justices seems important here. We can't have clowns on the Court.

General: Of course not. But their authority is by law; it's not simply personal.

Director: But when they first ruled a law unconstitutional, they broke new ground. People were divided on whether they had the authority to do so. The personal authority of those on the Court helped carry the day. And I bet if we looked hard enough, we could find other important examples of personal authority rising high like this.

Politician: That's absolutely true. Too bad we don't have a historian here with us now.

General: So what's the point? That it's murky at the heights of authority, with personal authority and legal authority mingling?

Politician: Don't let me disillusion you General, but law is inherently political. The Justices talk a good game to the contrary, but they know this truth in their hearts. And if they don't, that makes for trouble, in my expert opinion.

Director: What's the trouble?

Politician: Sometimes laws need to be fudged a little—for good reason. But true believers won't let that happen, even though they agree the consequences will be bad or unjust.

General: Even I know that. Sometimes a good interpretation can save the day. But that makes law political? To my mind, it just makes law... human.

48

Director: So inhuman law is bad.

Politician: Of course it's bad. Anything 'inhuman' is bad.

General: I love my dog. Are you saying he's bad?

Politician: Dogs are 'non-human', not 'inhuman'.

Director: But isn't the effect the same when it comes to laws? Non-human, inhuman—what does it matter? Anything but human is what we're against.

Politician: Can you imagine me running on a humanity platform?

Director: I can. It ties in nicely with healthcare, no?

Politician: Yes, I think it does. I'll have to give it some thought. But let's snap back to our present plight. What's the forecast?

General: I'll go over and see.

Politician: My, it's gotten late. But I'm not tired.

Director: Neither am I. Why do you think that is?

Politician: Good conversation. It's better than coffee, or any other drug.

General: It's going to be bad for a while. We're lucky if we get out late tomorrow.

Politician: I hate working from hotel rooms during the day.

Director: Maybe the three of us could rent a conference room.

Politician: That's a great idea! But I'll warn you, I'm very loud on the phone.

General: That's no problem for me. I'm used to noisy environments. I can do most of my work on my computer.

Director: So can I. I just have one conference call, but I'm only listening in.

Politician: Too many people just listen in to calls, if you ask me. It seems like a waste of time. What's the call?

Director: My boss is explaining something to his boss and his boss's peers.

Politician: Why does he want you there?

Director: So I can debrief him and make follow-up recommendations.

Politician: Sounds like you should be your boss.

Director: I'm not ambitious that way.

Politician: Why not?

Director: I have other ambitions.

Politician: Let me guess. Having more conversations like this.

Director: Yes.

Politician: I think that's a sign of decay—someone with your abilities declining to put them to better use.

Director: But I do put them to better use.

Politician: Why don't you want to rise?

Director: Rise where? My boss is firmly in place. I can hardly leap-frog him. So it seems I'm where I am for now.

Politician: Oh, just shake things up and you might be surprised to see it turn out well for you.

Director: I do shake things up. But nothing much changes with my boss and me.

Politician: You said you put your abilities to better use. You're talking about philosophy, right?

Director: I am.

General: Director, I know what you mean. But I agree with Politician. Philosophy is a sign of decay.

Director: In the individual?

General: No, not at all. In society. How can a good society not give someone like you a good place?

Director: I have a good place.

General: Yes, yes—but not as good as you should.

Director: I like my job, more or less. Is that so bad?

General: When your ambition, which I suspect was once great, is limited to friendly conversation—something is wrong. Not with you! Please know this isn't an attack on you. It's an attack on those who could help you but don't.

Director: I'm not looking for any help. Besides, they don't help because they don't think I'm a 'good fit'.

Politician: Ah, the old not-a-good-fit. Funny how you can be an authority on philosophy, but not-a-good-fit everywhere else.

Director: And I'm not even an authority on philosophy!

Politician: Then I'm afraid you're useless! Ha, ha!

General: Oh, he doesn't mean it. I'm certain you do very well in your operations job.

Director: Thank you. I'd say I do pretty well.

General: Your boss certainly has confidence in you.

Director: That he does.

Politician: Let me guess. You have authority-to with your boss.

Director: Yes.

Politician: While he has authority-over with you.

Director: True, but he doesn't exercise it much. He mostly treats me as a friend.

General: When does he exercise it?

Director: When he's stressed.

Politician: That's always the way. Friends until someone turns up the heat. How can you stand it?

Director: I try to keep the heat away.

Politician: Listen to you! You're the best employee there is. You shield your boss from heat—in addition to everything else!

Director: I try my best to be of use.

Politician: I take it back. You're not useless at all. I want you on my team.

Director: But I'm loyal to my boss. He really is a friend, despite his moments. Besides, what would I do on your team?

Politician: Keep the heat from me.

Director: I don't know your kind of heat.

Politician: Somehow I think you'd learn very quickly. You can be my director of operations. And what that means we'll keep vague, so you can have broader scope.

Director: That's tempting. But what about philosophy? My boss is tolerant here.

Politician: I'm afraid there won't be much time for that. Things happen at a greater speed in the capital.

Director: Do they? I thought they often got mired in muck and slowed to a crawl.

Politician: Yes, for some things. But while legislation is crawling people are scrambling behind the scenes. It's never slow. Re-election is every two years. There's always urgent work to be done.

Director: Then I'm not sure. I can't live blizzard to blizzard as far as philosophy goes. I need time.

Politician: You'd rather have philosophical conversations than be on the team that changes the nation for good?

Director: If it's a simple yes or no choice? Yes, I'll choose philosophy every time.

General: Director, you don't need hours of time like tonight, do you? Can't you have philosophy in ten minutes alone?

Director: It's possible, though not optimal. But maybe....

Politician: Maybe what?

Director: Lobbyists. They always want something from you.

Politician: Oh, if you could get them out of my hair that would be a blessing.

Director: Maybe some of them are open to philosophy.

Politician: Yes, and they would spend as much time with you as you want!

Director: And they're among the brightest of the bright?

Politician: Some of them are, sure.

Director: I like having conversations with the brightest of the bright.

Politician: Well, there you are!

Director: And I would have a sort of authority-over with them. They want something I've got—your ear.

Politician: I see you're warming to the idea.

Director: Yes, but they might be too hungry.

Politician: What's wrong with hungry?

Director: They might be hungry for money and humor me and whatever I say.

Politician: Then refuse all meetings with them. Only take the ones where you really connect.

Director: You mean that?

Politician: Sure. I wouldn't meet with any of them if I had my choice. With you as my gatekeeper I feel confident I won't be wasting my time. I, too, like those who are open to philosophy.

Director: Why?

Politician: They're both flexible and astute. Screen them for me. And I will be glad.

Director: That I can no doubt do.

49

Politician: So is it settled? You'll come work for me?

Director: There is the small matter of what I'll be paid.

Politician: I'll match whatever you're currently at.

General: Cheapskate!

Politician: Government jobs pay less. To match is to exceed.

Director: Still, I'm loyal to my boss.

Politician: Consult to him on the side—without interfering with your work for me.

Director: I can do that.

General: Politician, I hope you're ready to adopt full authority-to. Director will accept no less.

Politician: Of course I'm ready. I want authority-to with him.

Director: Why?

Politician: I need an equal to ensure I haven't come off the tracks. You will help me see.

Director: I could ride out ahead on all the issues of the day and we'll see where I come off.

Politician: That would be valuable intelligence. I could see what to avoid and what to take more carefully.

General: So Director will clear a minefield for you.

Politician: Why not?

General: Director, is that what you want to do?

Director: It depends. What are the mines?

Politician: People who won't come around.

Director: And I'll try to make them come around—to your point of view, I assume.

Politician: Yes.

Director: And if I can't?

Politician: That's important to know.

General: So Director has to agree with your point of view.

Politician: Of course he does—as expressed here tonight.

Director: What if I only agree in part?

Politician: I expect nothing less. We just have to be open about where we disagree. We'll work out the rest.

Director: General, what do you think?

General: I think you'd be trading a dull job for one with some excitement. There's nothing wrong with that.

Director: And what do I tell my boss?

Politician: He'll understand.

Director: Can I give him four weeks' notice?

Politician: Two is standard.

Director: Yes, but he'll need time to adjust.

Politician: Well, I'd be a fool of a boss for preventing an employee from treating his old boss well. Take your four weeks. I'll have the paperwork sent to you tomorrow.

General: So it's done.

Politician: It's done. How do you feel, Director?

Director: A little nervous but good.

Politician: That's only natural. I think we'll do great things!

Director: Just send me the most difficult people and I'll do well.

Politician: I don't doubt you will. We'll be clearing the way.

General: What makes someone difficult in your line of work?

Politician: They want too much and offer too little.

General: And Director will make that clear?

Politician: Yes.

Director: I'll make clear the price of all things.

Politician: Well, not all things.

Director: Only the things that are for sale?

Politician: Ha, ha. Sure.

General: But really, Politician. What's for sale?

Politician: You really need this all spelled out?

General: I do.

Politician: Votes.

General: Votes are for sale?

Politician: Not 'sale' as in bribes. Sale as in trading for influence. Representative X wants funds for a highway project in her district. I offer to give her my vote provided she votes for healthcare down the road. There's nothing wrong with that. It's business as usual, friend. Director can lay this all out for me, so I don't have to waste my time.

General: And what do you do? Keep a spreadsheet of favors you owe and have owed?

Politician: Yes, as a matter of fact. I do.

General: So you're an authority on favors.

Politician: As Director will be, too. That's how things get done.

50

Director: Will I have any authority with these people?

Politician: The politicians? It all depends.

Director: On what?

Politician: How well you perform your job.

Director: I take it I won't have any authority-over, just authority-to.

Politician: That's only fitting, don't you think?

Director: I do. But I should make something clear. Authority-to tends to undermine authority-over.

Politician: My authority-over? How so?

Director: The people I deal with might develop authority-to with me. Then we're equals, more or less.

General: Why would that undermine Politician?

Director: He might no longer be in control.

General: Authority-to trumps authority-over?

Director: If given free choice? Every time.

Politician: Then that's a fine excuse for me to develop authority-to, as well.

General: I think that's good. If you can persuade, by means of authority-to, someone to help your cause, you'll likely have a willing helper. But if you persuade by means of authority-over....

Politician: Yes, I take the point.

Director: Not so fast. Those under authority-over are often very willing helpers.

General: But you just said authority-to always trumps authority-over.

Director: Yes, when given free choice. Choice is not often free.

General: But then it's not really choice.

Director: Agreed.

Politician: No, no—choice is always free, and we always have a choice. Always.

Director: What would you have us choose?

Politician: Greatness in our time.

General: I would love to see greatness—if it came with an acceptable risk.

Director: But what does greatness in government mean? Giving the People what they want?

Politician: Why, yes. What else? Do you deny they want healthcare?

Director: Many want government help with healthcare—and many don't, as we've said.

Politician: But the majority is what counts.

Director: When you're counting like that, popular majorities rule.

General: How else would we count?

Politician: He's hinting that we challenge the belief in one-man-one-vote.

General: I didn't know that was a belief. That just... is!

Politician: It hasn't always been that way.

General: Who would get more than one vote?

Politician: It depends on how you want to balance things. The rich might, the 'priesthood' might, those who inherit the vote might. It all depends.

General: Well, that sounds like a stupid thing to me.

Politician: And it gets stupider still. Some have had the right to veto all the others.

General: I don't doubt there are many ways to organize a government. But we should concern ourselves only with what concerns us.

Politician: And our concern is that Senate terms last two years, in order to make Senators more responsive to popular will.

General: That will have a destabilizing effect.

Politician: Not when the popular will is stable.

Director: Is it stable?

Politician: Concerning healthcare, it is.

General: And when the People thirst for war?

Politician: We'll likely have war.

General: A six-year senator might wait out the storm. A two-year senator can't.

Politician: Like I said, we'll have war—or not. It all depends.

Director: Charismatic personalities will have great effect, no?

Politician: Yes, and I am one.

Director: Can you sway a People bent on a particular course?

Politician: Temper them a bit, maybe. But sway them completely around? That would be hard and rare.

Director: But we believe the People know what's best.

Politician: Best for them, yes.

Director: Should we be concerned with anything else?

General: We three are part of the People, so whatever concerns us should be a concern for them.

Politician: That would be nice. But we are servants of the People—including you, Director, when you join my team.

Director: But there's something I have a hard time understanding. While in office, you have authority-over with them—you pass the laws that bind them. They, on the other hand, only have authority-over with you every two years when they vote.

Politician: Yes, I suppose that's true.

Director: Why do you think they put up with that?

Politician: That's how the system works.

Director: Wouldn't they rather have authority-over all the time?

Politician: Some would; some wouldn't.

Director: Why wouldn't they?

Politician: They don't want the responsibility.

Director: But some do.

Politician: Sure, some do.

Director: Should we give it to them?

Politician: If they vote an amendment, yes.

Director: And they could take responsibility via their computers, or phones, or whatever. Direct democracy.

General: That would be chaos. We need cooler heads to prevail, not the mob.

Director: The People are a mob?

General: Any people can be stirred, under the right circumstances, into a mob. The Founders of our country knew this. That's why we have representative, not direct, democracy.

Director: But Politician, you're open to it either way?

Politician: Representative or direct? Either way I'll have my place and do what I can to prevent a mob from forming.

Director: And if you determine you need more authority-over than -to?

Politician: I'll do what needs to be done.

51

Director: There are those who say we have representative democracy in order to preserve the interests of the rich. What do you think about that?

Politician: There's truth in it, of course. But I really think it's meant to prevent mob rule.

General: I agree. There's truth in it about the rich. When mobs rule, the rich are among the first to go. But mobs are no good for anyone—including those who start them.

Director: Do mobs have any authority?

General: They can arrogate authority for a time. But it's not true authority, and it can't last.

Politician: Oh, it can last—for years of hell. Nothing is worse than the authority-over of a mob.

Director: Not even a tyrant's authority-over?

Politician: That's usually how mob rule comes to an end—with the birth of a tyranny.

Director: General, you've seen both mob rule and tyranny at first hand. Which is worse?

General: Mob rule is more chaotic. Tyrannical rule is more deadly. Both are bad, in different ways.

Politician: Which would you prefer, Director?

Director: 'Prefer' seems too strong a word for how I'd feel. But there must be something about tyranny since people choose it to end mob rule.

Politician: 'Choose' is too strong a word for what they do. I'm sure they feel they have no choice.

Director: So they're stuck. How do they get out?

General: Foreign invasion is sometimes the way.

Director: The invaders restore the old authority?

General: They try, but it doesn't usually work very well.

Politician: So they set up a new government, one designed to meet the circumstances at hand.

Director: Is this an authority-to type government?

Politician: Ideally, yes. But the problem is there might not be authority-to on the other end.

Director: There is no People; only people.

Politician: Only people, yes.

Director: What does it take to turn a people into a People?

Politician: In our case it was historical luck coupled with the right leaders at the right time.

Director: So barring a lot of luck, there's not much we can do?

General: I've seen the attempt at turning people into People. I believe it does take a whole lot of luck for the right circumstances. Absent that, you have to settle for second best.

Director: If it weren't so late, I'd like to discuss that second best.

General: Yes, it really is late. I should turn in to bed. Tomorrow will be as busy as tonight was relaxing.

Politician: Agreed.

Director: I just have to check in with my boss.

Politician: You haven't done that yet?

Director: I sent a quick note saying how things went. He'll want more detail. I'll write it up and then turn in.

General: I suppose I should scan my messages to make sure nothing important came up. But like I said, they know how to reach me if anything critical arose.

Director: Then take the night off. I'm sure you deserve it. Get some much needed rest.

General: You know? I think I will. This has been an interesting evening. I've never talked philosophy like this.

Politician: That was philosophy? I thought it was politics.

General: You think everything is politics, so that's no surprise.

Politician: Director thinks everything is philosophy, so I wouldn't be surprised to hear him say that's all we talked.

Director: We spoke a mixture of politics and philosophy tonight. Which was the stronger element, who can say?

General: They're each strong in their own way. But since I'm officially outside of politics, I'm compelled to side with Director!

Politician: And since I'm officially inside politics, I'm compelled to side with myself. Where do you side, Director?

Director: With philosophy, of course.

Politician: So you side with yourself like me?

Director: In a sense. But I also side with a cause greater than myself.

Politician: But, really, so do I. So does General. So we do all three.

Director: Then on that I'll say goodnight.

General: Goodnight.

Politician: Until we meet again. We will meet again, won't we?

Director: You were serious about my working for you?

Politician: Quite serious.

Director: My boss will be shocked. He won't believe me unless I show him the paperwork from you.

Politician: That's none of his business. But it's fine if you want to show him that. My only concern is that he'll want to make a counter-offer.

Director: Money isn't my concern. I have enough for what I need. Philosophy is my concern. A role with you would give me broader scope.

General: And it's philosophy first, loyalty to Politician second?

Politician: I can live with that. But be careful, Director.

Director: Oh? Why?

Politician: Because politics is a bug that bites when you least expect it. And the fever it gives can change your course in life.

Director: I'd ask that bug on what authority it stands. And if the answer it gives doesn't satisfy me, I'd bite it back—and give it the only true change in course of life there is.

General: What true change is that?

Director: The change to philosophy, and its life of light.

Politician: Light, yes, but also contrast and shade.

Director: But that, my friend, goes without saying. So let's say no more but goodnight.

Politician: You really think you'll steal the last word from a politician?

Director: I had small hope.

Politician: Well, I hate to dash that hope; but do let me say to you both, with final authority on this stolen evening—goodnight.

Printed in the United States
by Baker & Taylor Publisher Services